ONE HUNDRED
BALLADES, RONDEAUX AND VIRELAIS
FROM THE LATE MIDDLE AGES

ONE HUNDRED
BALLADES, RONDEAUX
AND VIRELAIS
FROM THE LATE MIDDLE AGES

EDITED BY

NIGEL WILKINS

Lecturer in French
University of St Andrews

CAMBRIDGE
AT THE UNIVERSITY PRESS
1969

Published by the Syndics of the Cambridge University Press
Bentley House, 200 Euston Road, London N.W.1
American Branch: 32 East 57th Street, New York, N.Y.10022

© Cambridge University Press 1969

Library of Congress Catalogue Card Number: 69-10342

Standard Book Number: 521 07146 1

Printed in Great Britain
at the University Printing House, Cambridge
(Brooke Crutchley, University Printer)

CONTENTS

PREFACE

The purpose of this anthology is to give a clear demonstration of the value and interest of the three dominating forms in French lyric poetry in the fourteenth and fifteenth centuries, the *formes fixes* of the ballade, the rondeau and the virelai. It is true that, especially later in the fifteenth century, a number of sterile and artificial poems were written and that certain schools over-exploited the possibilities of technical tricks in composition; but to condemn *all* late medieval French lyric verse as empty and artificial, as is so often done, to pass it over as unworthy of consideration in anthologies, which is far from unknown—this is a gross and sad injustice. One of the main reasons for prejudice against poetry from this period seems to be ignorance on the part of critics: despite the excellent study of the poetry of this period recently published by Daniel Poirion, texts of even the greatest poets are often hard to obtain and there is no comprehensive collection gathering together the finest compositions of the time and showing the development of the *formes fixes* both in form and in subject-matter over two centuries. This is what the present anthology aims to do. The texts, which have been specially chosen to illustrate the diversity of themes and structure, have been standardised, but are based on the main published editions. They proceed in a generally chronological order, from poet to poet or group of poets, from Jehan de Lescurel and Jehan Acart de Hesdin at the very beginning of the fourteenth century, through the dominating figure of Guillaume de Machaut and the generation of minor poet-musicians following him in the mid- and late fourteenth century, to the non-musical poems of Jean le Seneschal in *Le Livre des Cent Ballades*, of Jehan Froissart and of Eustache Deschamps. Christine de Pisan follows, leading us into the fifteenth century, where we find Alain Chartier, a group of musicians still composing their own lyric texts, and, finally, Charles d'Orléans. Each section of poems is preceded by a brief commentary, and a select bibliography is provided after the musical examples.

N. W.

INTRODUCTION

It is common knowledge that the Provençal troubadours and the northern trouvères, from the eleventh to the thirteenth centuries, generally com-posed both poetry and music, setting their completed texts as songs to be performed sometimes by a soloist, sometimes by a group of singers, usually with the added decorative accompaniment of plucked or bowed string in-struments and often also with small drums, chimes and wind instruments.

In the past romance scholars have, with very few exceptions, paid little heed to the musical notes underlying the verses and in so doing have completely missed at least half of the originally intended effect. The early forms, the *Canzo,* the *Alba,* the *Pastorella,* the *Chansons de Toile,* the *Chansons de Croisade,* and many of the later ballades, rondeaux and virelais, were not meant to be recited or declaimed, let alone rest between the covers of a dusty book: they were meant to be performed in concert, brilliantly, dramatically.

Most of the recent impetus towards balanced editions of both poetry and music has come, perhaps not surprisingly, from the side of the musicologists, for they are generally better equipped to deal with the verses than are literary historians to grapple with the music. This may in turn explain why the best of such recent editions are concerned more with the lyric production of the *late* middle ages, for the musical aspects of the later period are in many ways especially absorbing and exciting, due mainly to the development of polyphony from the thir-teenth century (the simultaneous performance of different melodic lines in several voices or instruments) and the tremendous contemporary advance in the techniques of musical notation. Previously the musical settings, in secular works at least, were mainly monodic (a single melody) and the rhythmic notation vague and restrictive.

All too often it is imagined that the troubadour-trouvère tradition petered out with the end of the thirteenth century—with the great Adam de la Hale, perhaps.[1] Adam de la Hale, though, who himself made

---

[1] A new, modern transcription of both text and music of Adam's works is now available: N. Wilkins, *The Lyric Works of Adam de la Hale: Chansons, Jeux-Partis, Rondeaux, Motets* (*Corpus Mensurabilis Musicae* 44, American Institute of Musicology, 1967).

polyphonic settings, was pointing forward, an inspiration to later times, not the culmination of previous ages. One name towers over the four‑teenth century in lyric poetry, the unjustly neglected Guillaume de Machaut, virtuoso poet and musician; but even after Machaut, at the very end of the fourteenth century, there was yet another generation of skilled poet‑musicians, originating mostly in the north, but working mainly in the south, at the papal court of Avignon, in the royal court of Barcelona, or at Orthez in the service of Gaston Phébus, comte de Foix. In the hands of these late fourteenth‑century trouvères, musical composition attained an ingenuity and complexity unrivalled until our own times. Despite an immediate reaction, to relative simplicity in the early fifteenth century, this momentary cult of complexity in music must surely have been one of the main contributing factors to the divorce be‑tween poets and musicians which became confirmed at this time. Early poets are known who did *not* set their verses to music, of course, and a large part of Machaut's lyric output, especially his collection entitled *La Louange des Dames,* is without music; but when musical composition attained such a degree of complexity, *only* skilled professionals could manipulate their musical materials and henceforward no major poet could master this double art. Deschamps, Froissart, Christine de Pisan, Alain Chartier, Charles d'Orléans, François Villon—none of these outstand‑ing literary figures is known to have set his verses to music, though on occasion others did. From then on, musicians could still write verses and set them themselves, but pure poets had to be content with verses alone.

Apart from the pleasure which can be derived from the music, which is very varied in character, it is not possible fully to appreciate the structure and history of the ballade, rondeau and virelai forms without taking it into consideration. A few examples have been provided with the present edition to show the nature of the musical settings (where they apply), but the reader is urged to seek their closer acquaintance, by consulting the editions referred to, by listening to recordings or, best of all, by attempting to perform some himself.

In the fourteenth and fifteenth centuries in France, especially from Machaut onwards, lyric poetry was dominated by three basic forms, the ballade, the rondeau and the virelai.[1] The ballade dominated the four‑

---

[1] The Italian *Trecento* was likewise dominated by three *formes fixes* in secular music, the Madrigal, the Ballata and the Caccia; it is interesting to note that, as in France, pre‑

teenth century until the very close, but then almost disappeared, in the musical context at least, due to the immense popularity of the rondeau in the fifteenth century. The virelai, often similar to the caccia in the nature of its text, though more akin to the Italian ballata in structure, was fairly scarce.

Each form was subject to a certain amount of variation, but fundamentally was based on two sections of music shown in the schemata below and in the notes by the Roman figures I and II. In the edition, line numbers are deliberately placed against the text to indicate the underlying musical structure and indicate the beginning of one or the other of these two main divisions, which are easily recognizable in the music examples, being separated by a thick double-bar line, usually approximately halfway through the composition. The letters a b c d etc. in the schemata represent both the lines of verse and the rhyme scheme in the normal way. Capital letters A B C D represent refrain lines (A rhymes with a etc.). The numbers after each line-rhyme letter indicate the number of syllables in that line.

BALLADE: the fundamental musical pattern is I I II.
Example: Machaut's 'Quant Theseus, Hercules et Jason' (poem 18)
Music: I   I   II
Text: $a_{10}b_{10}$ $a_{10}b_{10}$ $c_7c_{10}d_{10}D_{10}$

The basic pattern is repeated for all subsequent stanzas (there are normally three) with the refrain line repeated at the end of each stanza. Sometimes there is no refrain line, as for example where an acrostic is involved, but this is rare. A varying number of lines may be set to either music section, though it is more usual to set two lines only to the first section, making four lines with the repeat. A basic rule for all the forms is that lines of text set to the same music section must have identical metrical and rhyme schemes. Within the basic form the number of lines may vary, as may rhyme and metre.

Guillaume de Machaut is generally considered to have established the ballade form as it is found in the latter part of the fourteenth century and his own examples show great versatility of approach. All the

ference changed as time progressed. In Italy taste favoured the madrigal above all in the early and middle part of the century, but changed to a bias towards the ballata in the later years. The caccia was comparatively rare.

fourteenth-century *formes fixes* can be identified earlier, though, for example in the works of the gifted young Parisian poet, Jehan de Lescurel. A development later in the century is the adoption of the ballade form by non-musician poets, who generally added an *envoi* of three or four lines after the last stanza. The ballade with *envoi*, modelled on the *chanson royal*, is found almost to the exclusion of the normal type in the works of Eustache Deschamps, John Gower, Christine de Pisan, Alain Chartier and Charles d'Orléans.

RONDEAU: the fundamental musical pattern is I II I I I II I II.
Example: Anon. 'Passerose de Biauté pure et fine' (poem 32)
Music: I   II   I I   I II   I   II
Text: $A_{10}B_{10}$ $a_{10}A_{10}$ $a_{10}b_{10}$ $A_{10}B_{10}$
In the late thirteenth and early fourteenth centuries fairly elaborate versions of this structure were common, but in the late fourteenth century the basic eight-line form was the most current. Later, elaboration returned, especially in the hands of Christine de Pisan, who shortened the repetitions of the refrains, and sixteen- and twenty-one-line types became popular.

VIRELAI: the fundamental musical pattern is I II II I (I).
Example: Jehan de Lescurel's 'Dis tans plus qu'il ne faudroit flours'
(poem 5)
Music: I   II   II   I   I
Text: $A_8B_8A_8B_8$ c_7d_7 c_7d_7 $a_8b_8a_8b_8$ $A_8B_8A_8B_8$ etc.
The text contained within this framework was extremely flexible, sometimes almost chaotic. The reason for this may be that the virelai, especially the 'realistic' type, often sought to paint vividly some scene of action, rather as in the Italian caccia, but perhaps more like the earlier French chace. The depiction of people rushing to a fire or of birds warbling in a thicket could only be 'realistic' if it was spontaneous, which sometimes seems almost to have excluded formal precision in the structure of the text.

This is the bare framework of the structural problem. The subtleties of changing taste and new experiment are discussed in detail in the notes, which form an essential part of the present study and are best read in historical progression.

It would be mistaken to give the impression that the ballades, rondeaux and virelais are interesting only in an academic way, for the mathematics of their construction. The themes treated in them are varied, and although the traditional elements of the courtly love lyric are very common, originality, depth of feeling and sense of humour are all to be found.

The love situation itself presents many facets: a number of poems simply present the lover's appeal to his lady

> *Douce dame, je vous pri,*
> *Faites de moi vostre ami.* (poem 3)

He needs her help

> *Faciez moi secours* (poem 4)

and begs her to have pity on him and to have mercy (poems 6, 7, 66, 67) or even just to let him see her

> Si ne vuelliez estre lente...
> De moy vëoir (poem 75)

All too often the lover is depicted as dying or suffering grievously; only his lady can save him

> *Ne me laissiez du tout mourir.* (poem 93)

The symptoms of the amorous malady are in evidence

> ...mon vis taint
> Et destaint
> Souvent de pluseurs coulours. (poem 16)

Only a lady doctor will do

> Et vous plaise estre le mire
> De mon mal. (poem 66)

The mental anguish is clear to see

> *Triste plaisir et doulereuse joie,*
> *Aspre doulceur, reconfort ennuyeux* (poem 78)

and yet

> *Que me vault donc le complaindre?* (poem 71)

Our collection does include, however, some direct *complaintes,* such as the two in virelai form by Machaut, where the lady is said to be

> *Plus dure qu'un dyamant*
> *Ne que pierre d'aÿmant* (poem 24)

and to cause the poet unnecessary suffering

> *Je n'ay mie desservi*
> *Qu'enhaï*
> *M'ait si*
> *Vos cuers . . .* (poem 25)

All the same, if the poet must die for love, it is a pleasant death

> Mourir ne puis plus doucement (poem 1)

and several poems stress a positive *need* for suffering in a love match

> *On se doit souffrir et taire*
> *Et tout en gré recevoir*
> *Quanqu'Amours ordonne, voir.* (poem 41)

> Car qui loyaument
> Veulent acquester
> Bon guerdonnement,
> Maint mal endurer
> Leur fault . . . (poem 90)

Often the lover feels that he is caught in a trap

> Pris fui en douce samblance (poem 8)

and certain poems, notably some by Charles d'Orléans, show a fear of being caught

> *Crevez moy les yeulx*
> *Que ne voye goutte,*
> *Car trop je redoubte*
> *Beaulté en tous lieulx.* (poem 96)

It is Charles d'Orléans who, maintaining the medical imagery, boasts that he has achieved immunisation against the pangs of love, through

> L'emplastre de Nonchaloir,
> Que sus mon cueur pieça mis. (poem 91)

Distance often intervenes, whether social or geographical, and the lover then laments that he is obliged

> *D'ainsy languir en estrange contrée.* (poem 26)

Because of this

> . . .eloignance
> Du très dous pays ou maint
> Celle qu'aim sanz decevance (poem 2)

time moves slowly and hangs heavy on the lover's hands

> Ce sejour m'anoie. (poem 42)

Again, only the lover's reunion with his lady will be able to console him

> *Jamais tant que je vous revoye,*
> *Ma très doulce dame et ma joye,*
> *Au cuer n'aray esbatement.* (poem 83)

There remain further traditional difficulties in the way of the lover and his lady who, after all, are an adulterous pair: the *mesdisans,* jealous gossip-mongers, are never far away (poem 85) and secrecy is an essential ingredient in the courtly relationship. The need for loyalty, especially on the lover's part, is constantly stressed

> *Ou Loyauté ne repaire*
> *Nulz ne devroit esperer*
> *Qu'Amours y ait son repaire!* (poem 22)

The author of the *Livre des Cent Ballades* has much to say about the

> ...travaulx
> Qu'Amours fait à ceulx endurer
> Qui estre ne veulent loiaux (poem 43)

and the point is forcibly made in a rondeau by Grenon

> *Se je vous ay bien loyaulment améé,*
> *Plus c'onques mais vous ayme loiaulment.* (poem 84)

Quite apart from the obvious need for secrecy, the lover is often timid and afraid to declare his passion openly; he wishes

> *Que je l'aie sans rouver* (poem 15)

and tries to send a bird to make the declaration in his place (poem 35)! Machaut excellently depicts the lover's embarrassment, in a Chanson royal:

> ..ne mes yeux saouler
> Ne porroie jamais de li vëoir.
> Si s'en porroit aucuns apercevoir
> Et mesdire, dont tost perdre porroie
> Mon cuer, m'amour, m'esperance et ma joie. (poem 20)

But hope is nearly always there to fire the lover on

> Pour quoi je preing esperance
> Que vostre biautés amaint
> Pitié, tant que vos cuers m'aint. (poem 9)

The lady is, of course, generally depicted as a creature of grace and perfection, even if she does often seem to be standing on a pedestal, high above the supplicant poet. She is

> Jeune et belle et gracïeuse (poem 5)

> ...bonne en dis,
> Et mieudre en fais. (poem 10)

Many poems compare her to flowers:

> *Passerose de biauté pure et fine*
> *Et de bonté très douche fleur de lys* (poem 32)

> *Rose, lis, printemps, verdure,*
> *Fleur, baume et très douce odour,*
> *Bele, passés en douçour.* (poem 23)

Froissart tells us that

> *Sus toutes flours j'aime la margherite.* (poem 37)

Jehan de Lescurel sends his lady greetings

> *Dis tans plus qu'il ne faudroit flours*
> *A faire un mont jusques és ciex* (poem 5)

and Machaut does not fail to use the famous symbol of the rose (poem 11); Chartier, too, has a symbolic garden (poem 77).

The courtly love relationship is not the only one represented here. Can we sense a breath of intimacy in Charles d'Orléans' whispered

> Ung mot pour tous,
> Bas qu'on ne l'oye:
> *Le voulez vous*
> *Que vostre soye?* (poem 95)

Christine de Pisan above all celebrates the joys of happy married love

> Doulce chose est que mariage,
> Je le puis bien par moy prouver, (poem 61)

which seems to make her widow's grief on the death of her husband all the more sincere and heartbreaking

> Dueil engoisseux, rage desmesurée,
> Grief desespoir, plein de forsennement,
> Langour sanz fin, vie maleürée
> Pleine de plour, d'engoisse et de tourment. (poem 62)

This is comparable to Chartier's lament on the death of his lady

> Vie en langueur, telle est ma destinée,
> Quant je ne voy ma doulce dame en vie. (poem 76)

Sometimes, too, the lady unbends and shows she shares the poets' passion

> Or suis vostre; par droit m'avez acquise. (poem 69)

Other poems in our collection deal with specific themes such as the lady's eyes (poem 79) or kisses (poem 94). Occasionally we are allowed to eavesdrop on a conversation concerning a topic of love, whether it be the sweet exchanges between the lover and his lady

> Ma dame, à Dieu vous viens dire;
> Baisiez moy au departir
> Et m'acolez... (poem 70) (cf. poem 19)

or the bantering of Deschamps' young gallants

> Dont viens tu? — De vëoir m'amie.
> — Qu'i as tu fait? — Tout mon plesir. (poem 47)

That more than one approach to love was possible is clear from the invitation for *Responces* to the love debate of the *Livre des Cent Ballades* (poem 44). Some of the replies are distinctly satirical in tone, especially the duc de Berry's advice that in love

> *On peut l'un dire et l'autre doit on faire.* (poem 45)

The same tongue-in-the-cheek touch is present in Deschamps' scintillating portrait of a girl admiring her own perfection

> *Sui je, sui je, sui je belle?* (poem 60),

Christine de Pisan's mocking verses at the expense of the traditional doddering and ancient cuckold husband (poems 64, 65), or Dufay's regrets that his youth is past (poem 82).

And still there remain the 'realistic' type poems in which love becomes a battleground resounding to ferocious cries

> Wacarme, wacarme, quel dolour
> Et quel langour
> Suefre, dame, pour votre amour (poem 34),

where the nightingale sings

> *Hé, très doulz roussignol joly*
> *Qui dit occy, occy, occy* (poem 35),

where love is a fervent fire

> *Au feu! au feu! au feu! qui mon cuer art* (poem 80)

not even to be extinguished by the lover's tears

> *J'ay essayé par lermes à largesse*
> *De l'estaindre, mais il n'en vault que pis* (poem 88),

or where, as in Charles d'Orléans' allegorical ballade, a challenge is hurled down to the lover's dreaded opponent, *Dangier* (poem 89).

Allegory is a frequent and popular device, so often stemming from the celebrity of the *Roman de la Rose*. Charles d'Orléans has sleepless nights reading

> *Ou rommant de Plaisant Penser* (poem 87),

Fortune is an often encountered figure (poem 11).

Machaut especially displays a taste for mythological references and comparisons

> *Phyton, le mervilleus serpent*
> *Que Phebus de sa flesche occit* (poem 12),

but always to some purpose, as can amply be seen in the double ballade 'Ne quier vëoir la biauté d'Absalon / Quant Theseus, Herculès et Jason', where the poet dismisses all the famous exploits of the ancient heroes, since

> *Je voy assez, puis que je voy ma dame.* (poems 17 and 18)

Other poems in this anthology deal with a diversity of topics in no way connected with love, and here the poet has possibly greater scope for originality and often allows his personality to emerge more clearly. Machaut is represented by an amusing poem on his gout (poem 13) and a ballade giving the medieval colour symbolism (poem 14). But in the sphere of personal, non-amorous poetry, Eustache Deschamps reigns supreme: a whole world is here, ranging from his self-mockery

> *...Eustaces, qui a la teste tendre* (poem 46)

and grumbling about people who have borrowed his books and not returned them (poem 46) or his request to be allowed to retain his hat before his royal patron on account of the cold weather (poem 49), through his advice on how to avoid the plague

> Il doit courroux et tristece fuir,
> Laissier le lieu ou est la maladie (poem 56)

or the need for a man to travel and see the world

> *Il ne scet rien qui ne va hors* (poem 53),

his ballade in praise of Christine de Pisan (poem 57), his dark premonitions towards the end of his life

> *Hui est li temps de tribulacion* (poem 54)

with his musings on the *ubi sunt* theme (poem 59) or his masterly poem on old age

> Je deviens courbes et bossus,
> J'oÿ très dur, ma vie decline (poem 58),

to his political and historical ballades, a kind of chronicle of his times in verse (poems 48 and 55). His lament on the death of Machaut is a fitting epitaph for the master to whom he owed so much (poems 50 and 51).

There are other political poems or poems in praise of patrons in our collection (e.g. poems 27, 28 and 29); a rondeau in praise of the Virgin (poem 33); an extremely witty poem on being in a temper

> Puisque je sui fumeux plains de fumée (poem 30);

the poignant plight of Senleches and his fellow jongleurs, forced to set out wandering again after their patroness had died (poem 31); some moving poems by Charles d'Orléans showing the effects of his exile (poem 86), of old age (poem 99) and the *Ennui* which so disturbed him (poem 98); further works by the same poet include the ballade written for his Puy at Blois (poem 92), his famous

> *Le temps a laissié son manteau*
> *De vent, de froidure et de pluye* (poem 97)

and a poem on winter (poem 100); a couple of somewhat didactic poems by Froissart (poems 38 and 39); and finally a few *jeux d'esprit*, such

as Christine de Pisan's absurd little monosyllabic rondeau (poem 73)
or Machaut's number riddle

Dix et sept, cinq, trese, quatorse et quinse. (poem 21)

This is poetry well worth reading and, of course, where music is
involved, well worth hearing in performance. It is to be hoped that the
present anthology will help to revive interest in this important and
enjoyable aspect of the literature of France.

JEHAN DE LESCUREL

Jehan de Lescurel is known solely for thirty-four French lyric works set to music and contained in six leaves of the manuscript Paris, B.N., f.fr. 146. These works comprise fifteen ballades, twelve rondeaux, five virelais and two extended *dits* with interpolated refrains. Son of a wealthy bourgeois Parisian family, Lescurel was a student cleric at the cathedral of Notre Dame, but was hanged for rape in 1304. Perhaps the greatest importance of his work lies in its clear demonstration that the three secular lyric *formes fixes* were already settled and established by the very first years of the fourteenth century. Lescurel represents a vital link between the age of Adam de la Hale and that of Guillaume de Machaut and, moreover, is a sensitive and skilful artist in his own right.

⇥ 1 ⇤

ballade

    Amour, voulés vous acorder
2 Que je muire pour bien amer?
3 Vo vouloir m'esteut agréer;
    Mourir ne puis plus doucement.
        Vraiement,
    Amours, faciez voustre talent.

7 Trop de mauls m'esteut endurer
8 Pour celi que j'aim sanz fausser.
9 N'est pas par li, au voir parler,
    Ains est par mauparliere gent.
        Loiaument,
    Amours, faciez voustre talent.

13 Dous amis, plus ne puis durer
14 Quant ne puis ne n'os regarder
15 Vostre dous vis riant et cler.
    Mort, alegez mon grief torment;
        Ou, briefment,
    Amours, faciez voustre talent.

13

⇥ 2 ⇤

ballade

Comment que, pour l'eloignance
Du très dous pays ou maint
3 Celle qu'aim sanz decevance,
Aie souffert meschief maint,
5 L'espoir qu'ai, qu'encore m'aint
La doucette simple et coie,
Fait que mon cuer li remaint
Et que mon cors vit en joie.

Par ramembrer sa semblance
Me sens d'amer si ataint
11 Que mon cuer d'autre plaisance
N'a, ne de grief ne se plaint.
13 Le desir qui me remaint,
— Dex, si qu'à lesir la voie —
Fait que mon cuer li remaint
Et que mon cors vit en joie.

17 Souvent sens grief et pesance,
Que mon cuer que liés soit faint,
19 Par ce c'on n'ait connoissance
De quel mal le vis ai taint,
21 Ne qui la belle est, qui craint,
Pour qui Amours, où que soie,
Fait que mon cuer li remaint
Et que mon cors vit en joie.

☩ 3 ☩

rondeau

1 *Douce dame, je vous pri,*
2 *Faites de moi vostre ami.*
3 Belle, aiés de moi merci;
4 *Douce dame, je vous pri*
5 Qu'il soit ainsi com je di.
6 De cuer amoureus joli,
7 *Douce dame, je vous pri,*
8 *Faites de moi vostre ami.*

☩ 4 ☩

rondeau

    Douce desirrée,
2   *Faciez moi secours;*
Pour vous seuffre griés doulours.

4   Moult forment m'agrée,
5   *Douce desirrée,*
6   La douce pensée
7   Qui me croist touz jours
En esperant voz douçours:
9   *Douce desirrée,*
10   *Faciez moi secours;*
Pour vous seuffre griés doulours.

☩ 5 ☩

virelai

Dis tans plus qu'il ne faudroit flours
A faire un mont jusques és ciex
Mant à vous salus et douçours
Et veil d'amer moi vous doint Diex.

5   Jeune et belle et gracïeuse,
En vous ai tout mon cuer mis;
7   Honeur et joie amoureuse
Aiez, frans cuer dous, toudis.

9 Ne senz grietés, mes granz douçours
 Dés que vous remir de mes iex;
 En moi croit tout ainsi amours
 Loiaus puis par vous ai biens tiex.

13 *Dis tans plus qu'il ne faudroit flours*
 A faire un mont jusques és ciex
 Mant à vous salus et douçours
 Et veil d'amer moi vous doint Diex.

17 En fais et diz savoureuse,
  Sage dame au cors faitiz,
19 Car soiez douce et piteuse
  Vers moi qui sui voz amis.

21 Raisons veut que soie touz jours
 En vous servant cois et doutiex,
 Larges, courtois, si grans honours
 Vient de vous; pour ce, cuer gentiex,

25 *Dis tans plus qu'il ne faudroit flours*
 A faire un mont jusques és ciex
 Mant à vous salus et douçours
 Et veil d'amer moi vous doint Diex.

29 Or proi Amour que soigneuse
  Vers vous, doucete au cler vis,
31 Soit pour moi et curieuse
  Si que vo cuer soit espris

33 Aussi com sui et par tieux tours;
 Lors serai celans et soutiex
 Vers vous plus qu'ore et nuis et jours
 Et pour ce, pour plaire vous miex,

37 *Dis tans plus qu'il ne faudroit flours*
 A faire un mont jusques és ciex,
 Mant à vous salus et douçours
 Et veil d'amer moi vous doint Diex.

JEHAN ACART DE HESDIN

Jehan Acart was a *frère hospitalier* in Hesdin (Pas-de-Calais) in the early part of the fourteenth century. His interest for us here lies in an apparently youthful work, an allegorical love poem entitled *La Prise amoureuse,* composed in 1332, into which were interpolated a number of the lyric *formes fixes* (nine ballades and nine rondeaux). The unique source, manuscript Paris, B.N., f.fr. 24391, contains blank spaces left beneath the lyric texts for the music, but this was never written in.

The poet may be identical with the theologist Johannes de Hisdinio, known for several works in Latin later in the fourteenth century.

⊁{ 6 }⊁

ballade

Dés que je fui hors d'ignorance
Et que connui qu'estoit honnours,
3 Emprienta vo douce samblance,
Dame, en mon cuer loial amours.
5 Et je, qui ne pensoie aillours,
Liez à vous servir m'assenti,
Car en sens et bonté aussi
Vi bien qu'estïés par droiture
Flours de toute créature.

10 Or si reting celle plaisance,
Et fu en espoir mes retours
12 Qu'en cors, par si noble ordenance
Mené, fust pitiez et douçours;
14 Par coi j'ai mis sens, temps et jours
Pour acquerre l'otroi d'ami
Au gré de si noble merci
Comme de vous, qui estes pure
Flours de toute créature.

19 Pour ce, dame plaisans et franche,
   Ains que cheüs soit en decours
21 Mes cors par trop longue souffrance,
   Soit de moi pris aucuns boins tours,
23 Si qu'en pitié de vo secours
   Voie mon cors povre enrichi,
   Et des maus dont tant ai langui
   Me prenés par vo grace en cure,
   Flours de toute créature.

⋊{ 7 }⋉

ballade

Gens cors, en biauté parfais,
   Et par fais
Sus toutes dames parfaite,
4 Or sui je pris et atrais
   Par les trais
De vostre amoureuse atraite,
7 Si vuelliés de moi curer
   Et curer
Celui qu'en vous tout a mis,
Mort ou vie, comme amis.

11 Pour voir, si me plaist li fais,
   Si qu'à fais
Ne m'est l'attente; ains m'afaite
14 Que mos ne soit ja retrais
   Que retrais
Soie, et fust mercis retraite.
17 Ains vuel, tant com puis durer,
   Endurer
Ce qui par vous m'ert tramis,
Mort ou vie, comme amis.

21 Nepourquant seroit refais
Et refais
Mes cuers, se grace m'ert faite,
24 Qu'Amours se fust en vous trais,
Si qu'estrais
Fust l'otrois et merci traite;
27 Car adonc, sans reüser,
Porroie user
Es biens qu'Espoirs m'a pramis
Mort ou vie, comme amis.

8

rondeau

Par si plaisant atraiance
2 *M'a volu Amours atraire*
Que ja ne m'en quier retraire.

4 Pris fui en douce samblance
5 *Par si plaisant atraiance,*

6 Que je preing en la plaisance
7 Voloir de dire et de faire
Qui doie à tous amans plaire.

9 *Par si plaisant atraiance*
10 *M'a volu Amours atraire*
Que ja ne m'en quier retraire.

9

rondeau

En vostre douce samblance,
Dame, où toute biautés maint,
3 *Mes cuers loyaument remaint.*

4 C'est li tresors de plaisance
Où pris en ont esté maint,
6 *En vostre douce samblance,*
Dame, où toute biautés maint.

8   Pour quoi je preing esperance
    Que vostre biautés amaint
10 Pitié, tant que vos cuers m'aint.

11 *En vostre douce samblance,*
    Dame, où toute biautés maint,
13 *Mes cuers loyaument remaint.*

ᛈ 10 ᛁ

rondeau

    Tant est vos gens cors jolis,
     Ma dame, parfais
3 *Que du vëoir est cuers faillis*
     Refais.

5 Car bele estes, bonne en dis,
    Et mieudre en fais,
7 *Tant est vos gens cors jolis,*
    Ma dame, parfais.

    Ne n'ataint cors qui soit vis
    Au meneur des trais
11 Que Nature a en vo dous vis
    Pourtrais.

13 *Tant est vos gens cors jolis,*
    Ma dame, parfais
15 *Que du vëoir est cuers faillis*
    Refais.

GUILLAUME DE MACHAUT

Guillaume de Machaut, virtuoso poet and musician, is the dominating figure in French lyric poetry in the fourteenth century. Born *c.* 1300, he travelled widely in the service of Jean de Luxembourg, king of Bohemia. His large poetic output is preserved in several very elaborate and beautiful illuminated manuscripts, some apparently ordered according to Machaut's personal wishes (e.g. manuscripts Paris, B.N., f.fr. 1584–1586, f.fr. 22545–6).

In the lyric field his importance was not so much that of an innovator but as an elaborator; he experimented freely with the *formes fixes* and far surpassed his predecessors in the quality as well as in the quantity of his work, perhaps especially so in his music. Machaut gave the ballade, rondeau and virelai forms widespread popularity and after him they were to dominate the poetic scene until the dawn of the Renaissance in France, in the sixteenth century. Machaut's works include forty-two ballades, twenty-two rondeaux, thirty-three virelais, lais and motets set to music, while many further lyric pieces are found incorporated in his larger works and collections (e.g. *Le Livre du Voir Dit, Le Remède de Fortune*, and, above all, *La Louange des Dames*). His death in 1377 was greatly regretted, especially by his follower Eustache Deschamps.

⇥ 11 ⇤

ballade

De toutes flours n'avoit et de tous fruis
En mon vergier fors une seule rose:
3 Gastés estoit li surplus et destruis
Par Fortune qui durement s'opose
5   Contre ceste douce flour
Pour amatir sa coulour et s'odour.
Mais se cueillir la voy ou tresbuchier,
Autre aprés li ja mais avoir ne quier.

9 Mais vraiement ymaginer ne puis
Que la vertus, où ma rose est enclose,
11 Viengne par toy et par tes faus conduis,
Ains est drois dons naturex; si suppose
13   Que tu n'avras ja vigour
D'amanrir son pris et sa valour.
Lay la moy donc, qu'ailleurs n'en mon vergier
Autre aprés li ja mais avoir ne quier.

17 Hé! Fortune, qui es gouffres et puis
Pour engloutir tout homme qui croire ose
19 Ta fausse loy, où riens de bien ne truis
Ne de seür, trop est decevans chose;
21   Ton ris, ta joie, t'onnour
Ne sont que plour, tristece et deshonnour.
Se ti faus tour font ma rose sechier,
Autre aprés li ja mais avoir ne quier.

⨯{ 12 }⨯

ballade

Phyton, le mervilleus serpent
Que Phebus de sa flesche occit,
3 Avoit la longueur d'un erpent,
Si com Ovides le descrit.
5 Mais onques homs serpent ne vit
Si fel, si crueus ne si fier
Com le serpent qui m'escondit,
Quant à ma dame merci quier.

9 Il ha sept chiés, et vraiement,
Chascuns à son tour contredit
11 La grace, où mon vray desir tent,
Dont mes cuers en dolour languit:
13 Ce sont Refus, Desdaing, Despit,
Honte, Paour, Durté, Dangier,
Qui me blessent en l'esperit,
Quant à ma dame merci quier.

17 Si ne puis durer longuement,
     Car ma tres douce dame rit
19 Et prent deduit en mon tourment
     Et és meschiés, où mon cuers vit.
21 Ce me destruit, ce me murdrit,
     Ce me fait plaindre et larmoier,
     Ce me partue et desconfit,
     Quant à ma dame merci quier.

⇥13⇤

ballade

  Dou memoire des hommes degradés
  Et des livres, où il a esté mis,
3 Maudis de Dieu, de tous sains condampnés,
  De la clarté des estoiles bannis
5   Puis estre li mois de Mars
  Et de mal feu d'enfer brulés et ars,
  Li et si jours et sa puissance toute,
  Quant il m'a fait avoir en piet la goutte.

9 Dou biau soleil ne soit point alumés
  Ne de la lune esclairié ne servis,
11 Mais tenebreus soit et pleins d'obscurtés,
  Pour ce qu'il est à Nature annemis.
13   En bataille soit couars
  Et desconfis com ribaus et pillars,
  Avec le roy de glace que trop doubte,
  Quant il m'a fait avoir en piet la goutte.

17 Des autres mois soit desjoins et ostés
  Et de Nature oublïés et haÿs,
19 Et Avril soit exauciés, honnourés,
  Li biaus, li dous, li courtois, li jolis,
21   Que florist de toutes pars
  Les prez, les bois et les champs et les pars,
  Et me garist maugré Mars et sa route,
  Quant il m'a fait avoir en piet la goutte.

⊁14⊁

ballade

Qui de couleurs saroit à droit jugier
Et dire la droite signefiance,
3 On deveroit le fin azur prisier
Dessus toutes; je n'en fais pas doubtance.
5   Car jaune, c'est fausseté,
Blanc est joie, vert est nouvelleté,
Vermeil ardeur, noir deuil; mais ne doubt mie
Que fin azur loyauté signefie.

9 Si vueil amer l'azur et tenir chier
Et moy parer de li en ramembrance
11 De loyauté qui ne saroit trichier,
Et li porter honneur et reverence.
13   Car, en bonne verité,
Riens ne vaut chose, où il n'a verité,
N'il n'est amans qui ne tesmongne et die
Que fin azur loyauté signefie.

17 Si l'ameray de fin cuer et entier
Et porteray sans nulle difference,
19 Car moult me puet valoir et avancier
Et donner pais, joie et bonne esperence.
21   Et mes amis qui bonté
Ha dessus tous m'en sara trés bon gré;
Car il scet bien, entre amy et amie,
Que fin azur loyauté signefie.

✝15✝

Amours me fait desirer
    Et amer
De cuer si folettement
4 Que je ne puis esperer
    Ne penser
N'ymaginer nullement
7 Que le dous viaire gent
    Qui m'esprent
Me doie joie donner,
10 S'Amours ne fait proprement
    Telement
Que je l'aie sans rouver.

13 S'ay si dur à endurer
    Que durer
Ne puis mie longuement;
16 Car en mon cuer vueil celer
    Et porter
Ceste amour couvertement,
19 Sans requerre aligement,
    Qu'à tourment
Vueil miex ma vie finer.
22 Et si n'ay je pensement
    Vraiement
Que je l'aie sans rouver.

25 Mais Desirs fait embraser
Et doubler
Ceste amour si asprement
28 Que tout me fait oublier,
Ne penser
N'ay fors à li seulement;
31 Et pour ce amoureusement
Humblement
Langui sans joie gouster.
34 S'en morray, se temprement
Ne s'assent
Que je l'aie sans rouver.

⊁ 16 ⊀

ballade

Dous amis, oy mon complaint:
A toy se plaint
Et complaint,
Par defaut de tes secours,
5 Mes cuers qu'Amours si contraint
Que tiens remaint;
Dont mal maint
Ay, quant tu ne me secours
9 En mes langours
Car d'aillours
N'est riens qui confort m'amaint.
12 S'en croist mes plours
Tous les jours,
Quant tes cuers en moy ne maint.

15 Amis, t'amour si m'ataint
 Que mon vis taint
  Et destaint
Souvent de pluseurs coulours
19 Et mon dolent cuer estraint;
 Si le destraint
  Qu'il estaint
Quant en toy n'a son recours
23 S'a jours trop cours,
 Se n'acours
Pour li garir, car il creint
26 Mort qui d'Amours
  Vient le cours,
Quant tes cuers en moy ne maint.

29 Mon cuer t'amour si ensaint
 Qu'il ne se faint
  Qu'il ne t'aint
Pour tes parfaites douçours;
33 Et ta biauté qui tout vaint
 Dedens li paint
  Et empraint
Aveuc tes hautes valours.
37 S'en sont gringnours
  Mes dolours
Et plus dolereus mi plaint
40 Et en decours
  Mes vigours,
Quant tes cuers en moy ne maint.

✳ 17 & 18 ✳

double ballade

Ne quier vëoir la biauté d'Absalon
Ne d'Ulixès le sens et la faconde,
3   Ne esprouver la force de Sanson,
Ne regarder que Dalila le tonde,
5   Ne cure n'ay par nul tour
Des yeux Argus ne de joie gringnour,
Car pour plaisance et sanz aÿde d'ame
Je voy assez, puis que je voy ma dame.

9   De l'ymage que fist Pymalion
Elle n'avoit pareille ne seconde;
11   Mais la belle qui m'a en sa prison
Cent mille fois est plus bele et plus monde:
13   C'est uns drois fluns de douçour
Qui puet et scet garir toute dolour;
Dont cilz a tort qui de dire me blame:
Je voy assez, puis que je voy ma dame.

17   Si ne me chaut dou sens de Salemon,
Ne que Phebus en termine ou responde,
19   Ne que Venus s'en mesle, ne Mennon
Que Jupiter fist muer en aronde;
21   Car je di, quant je l'äour,
Aim et desir, ser et crieng et honnour,
Et que s'amour seur toute rien m'enflamme,
Je voy assez, puis que je voy ma dame.

✳ ✳ ✳

Quant Theseüs, Herculès et Jason
Cercherent tout, et terre et mer parfonde,
3   Pour acroistre leur pris et leur renom
Et pour vëoir bien tout l'estat dou monde,
5   Moult furent dignes d'onnour.
Mais quant je voy de biauté l'umble flour,
Assevis sui de tout, si que, par m'ame,
Je voy assez, puis que je voy ma dame.

9 Car en vëant sa biauté, sa façon
Et son maintieng qui de douceur seuronde,
11 J'y preng assez bien pour devenir bon,
Car le grant bien de li en moy redonde
13 Par grace de fine amour
Qui me contraint à haïr deshonnour
Et tout vice; si puis dire sanz blame:
Je voy assez, puis que je voy ma dame.

17 Vëoir ne quier la dorée toison
Ne les Yndes ne de Rouge Mer onde,
19 N'aus infernaus penre guerre ou tençon
Pour eslongier le regart de la blonde
21 Dont me vient joye et baudour
Et doulz penser; si tieng pour le millour
Qu'à tout conter et bien peser à drame,
Je voy assez, puis que je voy ma dame.

⊀ 19 ⊁

'*ballade double*'

'Dame plaisant, nette et pure,
Delitable à regarder,
3 Vo gracïeuse figure
Et vo doulz vïaire cler
5 Desir tant à remirer
Que tous mes scens s'en desvoie,
S'ainsi est que ne vous voie.'

8 'Se vostre dolour est dure,
Dous amis, à endurer
10 Sachiés que ma norriture
Est de pleindre et de plourer.
12 Einsi ne puis plus durer,
Ains desir que morte soie,
S'ainsi est que ne vous voie'.

15 'Helas! douce creature,
C'on ne porroit comparer,
17 Sentés vous dont la pointure
De vostre ami desirer?
19 Certes, or doit bien doubler
La dolour qui me maistroie,
S'ainsi est que ne vous voie.'

22 'Eimmi! elle m'est si dure,
Dous amis, loiaus, sans per,
24 Que toute m'envoiseüre
Et ma joie entroublier
26 Me fait; ne reconforter
Nullement ne me porroie,
S'ainsi est que ne vous voie.'

29 'Ma dame, or soiés seüre
Que je muir pour vous amer.
31 Car li desirs et l'ardure
Que j'ay de tost retourner
33 Vers vous me font desperer;
Si que jamais n'avray joie,
S'ainsi est que ne vous voie.'

36 'Amis, c'est dure aventure
Que Diex vuet à nous donner.
38 Mais ja mon cuer ne ma cure,
Mon desir ne mon penser
40 Ne verra nulz remuer,
Pour grieté qu'Amours m'envoie
S'ainsi est que ne vous voie.'

⇥ 20 ⇤

Onques mais nulz n'ama si folement
Com j'ay amé et com j'aim, sans cesser,
Qu'aler ne puis vers ma dame souvent,
Et quant je y sui, à li ne puis parler,
Ne je ne l'os vëoir ne regarder.
Et miex morir ameroie, pour voir,
Que par autrui li feïsse savoir
Comment je l'aim, car trop me mefferoie,
Se de m'amour en autrui me fioie.

10 Et nonpourquant je l'aim si sagement
C'on ne porroit plus sagement amer,
Ce m'est avis; se son cors le gent
A mon voloir pöoie remirer
Et vis à vis mes dolours demoustrer
Ou dire à li par autrui mon voloir,
Ce me porroit honnir et decevoir,
Et mettre ad ce qu'avent mes jours morroie
Ou que vëoir jamais ne l'oseroie.

19 Car je l'aim tant et si desiramment
Qu'ades vorroie aveuc li demourer
Et son parler, dont tel douceur descent
Qu'autre douçour ne s'i puet comparer,
Toudis oïr; ne mes yex saouler
Ne porroie jamais de li vëoir.
Si s'en porroit aucuns apercevoir
Et mesdire, dont tost perdre porroie
Mon cuer, m'amour, m'esperance et ma joie.

28 Dont me vaut miex amer celéement
Et mes dolours humblement endurer,
En atendant la mort ou aligement
D'Amours qui tant me scet nuire et grever,
Que tout perdre par maisement celer.
Si l'ameray, sans partir ne mouvoir,
De cuer, de corps, de penser, de povoir,
Tout mon vivant, sans ce que j'en recroie,
Et encor plus, se plus vivre povoie.

37 Si pri Amours, qui scet que loyaument
Et longuement l'ay servi, sans fausser,
Et serf encor de si vray sentement
Que tous me vueil en son service user,
Qu'elle pité face en ma dame ouvrer,
Tant que merci en puisse recevoir,
Ou que la mort me face tost avoir;
Car, par m'ame, s'à sa merci failloie
Devant la mort nulle riens ne vaurroie.

l'envoy

46 Princes, priez bonne Amour qu'elle m'oie,
Si que de li ne soie en nonchaloir,
Car je ne vueil ne desir autre avoir,
Fors tant, sans plus, que mors ou amés soie.

⋊21⋉

rondeau   *Dix et sept, cinq, trese, quatorse et quinse*
2   *M'a doucement de bien amer espris.*
3   Pris ha en moy une amoureuse emprise —
4   *Dix et sept, cinq, trese, quatorse et quinse —*
5   Pour sa bonté que chascuns loe et prise
6   Et sa biauté qui sur toutes a pris.
7   *Dix et sept, cinq, trese, quatorse et quinse*
8   *M'a doucement de bien amer espris.*

⭑⟨ 22 ⟩⭑

rondeau

    Où Loyauté ne repaire
2 *Nulz ne devroit esperer*
    Qu'Amours y ait son repaire;

4 N'amis vrais ne se doit traire
5 *Où Loyauté ne repaire,*

6 Ains s'en doit dou tout retraire,
7 Car trop en puet empirer,
    N'il ne porroit son preu faire.

9   *Où Loyauté ne repaire*
10 *Nulz ne devroit esperer*
    Qu'Amours y ait son repaire.

⭑⟨ 23 ⟩⭑

rondeau

    Rose, lis, printemps, verdure,
    Fleur, baume et tres douce odour,
3 *Bele, passés en douçour,*

4 Et tous les biens de Nature
    Avez, dont je vous äour.
6 *Rose, lis, printemps, verdure,*
    Fleur, baume et tres douce odour.

8 Et quant toute creature
    Seurmonte vostre valour,
10 Bien puis dire et par honnour:

11 *Rose, lis, printemps, verdure,*
    Fleur, baume et tres douce odour,
13 *Bele, passés en douçour.*

⊀ 24 ⊁

virelai

Plus dure qu'un dÿamant
Ne que pierre d'aÿmant
  Est vo durté,
Dame, qui n'avez pité
  De vostre amant
Qu'ociés en desirant
  Vostre amitié.

8 Dame, vo pure biauté
  Qui toutes passe, à mon gré,
    Et vo samblant
11 Simple et plein d'umilité,
  De douceur fine paré,
    En sousriant,

14 Par un acqueil attraiant,
  M'ont au cuer en regardant
    Si fort navré
  Que ja mais joie n'avré,
    Jusques à tant
  Que vo grace qu'il atent
    M'arez donné.

21 *Plus dure qu'un dÿamant*
  Ne que pierre d'aÿmant
    Est vo durté,
  Dame, qui n'avez pité
    De vostre amant
  Qu'ociés en desirant
    Vostre amitié.

28 J'ay humblement enduré
  L'amoureus mal et porté
    En attendant
31 Vostre bonne volenté
  Que j'ay en tous cas trouvé
    Dure et poingnant.

34 Et quant tous en vo commant
　　Suis, je me merveil comment
　　　　Vostre bonté
　　M'a sa grace refusé,
　　　　Quant en plourant
　　Vous ay et en souspirant
　　　　Merci rouvé.

41 *Plus dure qu'un dÿamant*
　　Ne que pierre d'aÿmant
　　　　Est vo durté,
　　Dame, qui n'avez pité
　　　　De vostre amant
　　Qu'ociés en desirant
　　　　Vostre amitié.

48 Helas! Dame, conforté
　　Ne m'avez en ma grieté,
　　　　Ne tant ne quant,
51 Eins m'avez desconforté,
　　Si que tout desconfort hé.
　　　　Mais nonpourquant

54 J'ameray d'or en avant
　　Plus fort qu'onques mais, et quant
　　　　Mort et miné
　　M'ara vostre cruauté
　　　　Qui m'est trop grant,
　　Lors sera bien apparant
　　　　Ma loyauté.

61 *Plus dure qu'un dÿamant*
　　Ne que pierre d'aÿmant
　　　　Est vo durté,
　　Dame, qui n'avez pité
　　　　De vostre amant
　　Qu'ociés en desirant
　　　　Vostre amitié.

⊁ 25 ⊁

virelai

     Dame, à qui
       M'ottri
   De cuer, sans penser laidure,
   Je n'ay mie desservi
     Qu'enhaï
      M'ait si
   Vos cuers qu'à desconfiture
   Soie pour l'amour de li.

9   Car de tres loial amour
     Maint jour
   Vous ay amé et servi,
12 N'onques vos cuers n'ot tenrour
     Dou plour
   Qui m'a tout anienti.

15   S'en gemi
     Et di
   Que ce n'est mie droiture
   Que toudis soie en oubli,
    Car en mi
     Par mi
   Partiroit mon cuer d'ardure,
   Bele, s'il estoit einsi.

23   *Dame, à qui*
     M'ottri
   De cuer, sans penser laidure,
   Je n'ay mie desservi
     Qu'enhaï
      M'ait si
   Vos cuers qu'à desconfiture
   Soie pour l'amour de li.

31 Helas! toudis sans sejour
    Äour
Vo doulz viaire joli,
34 Mais trouver n'i puis douçour
    N'amour
Fors samblance d'anemi.

37   S'en fremy,
    Aymi!
Et en dolour qui trop dure
Doleureusement langui,
    Quant meri
      D'ottri
Ne d'esperance seüre
Ne m'a encor esjoÿ.

45   *Dame, à qui*
    M'ottri
De cuer, sans penser laidure,
Je n'ay mie desservi
    Qu'enhaï
      M'ait si
Vos cuers qu'à desconfiture
Soie pour l'amour de li.

53 Belle et bonne, sans folour,
    D'onnour
Vous ha Diex si enrichi
56 Que vous estes de valour
    La flour;
Pour ce vous ay encheri.

59   Se vous pri
    Merci
Que de vostre grace pure
Me daingniés clamer ami;
    Et einsi
      Gari
M'arés dou mal que j'endure,
Tresdont que premiers vous vi.

67 *Dame, à qui*
   M'ottri
  De cuer, sans penser laidure,
  Je n'ay mie desservi
   Qu'enhaï
    M'ait si
  Vos cuers qu'à desconfiture
  Soie pour l'amour de li.

THE POST-MACHAUT
GENERATION

Machaut is often considered as the 'last of the trouvères', the culmination of the tradition of combined music and poetry which had originated
in eleventh-century Provence. In fact, however, a whole generation of
poet-musicians came after him, deeply indebted to him in verse forms
and ideas, but sometimes in conscious reaction against him in the
musical sphere.

Most of these late fourteenth-century poet-musicians, who emerged
from the early and mid-fourteenth-century Ars Nova and came to
exploit musical intricacies in an 'Ars Subtilior', as it is often called,
originated in the north but worked in the south, at the papal court in
Avignon or especially in the court of Gaston Phébus, comte de Foix,
in Orthez, or in the royal court of Barcelona.

P. des Molins was probably a Parisian who moved to Avignon about
1350 and again to Barcelona a few years later. He is known for two
ballades.

Magister Franciscus was probably a contemporary of Machaut but
is known to have worked in the court of Gaston Phébus. Two,
possibly three, ballades by him are known.

J. Cuvelier, known for four ballades, also wrote a lengthy epic-
chronicle, the *Vie du vaillant Bertrand du Guesclin,* between 1380 and
1387. He was not unknown in the court of Charles V of France, but
was no doubt employed in Orthez and also in Pamplona, in the
kingdom of Navarre.

Philipoctus de Caserta, known for six ballades and one rondeau as
well as for a short theoretical treatise, the *Regule Contrapuncti,* was
of south Italian origin, but must have learned the methods of 'ars subtilior' in Avignon in the 1380s. Later he was in the service of the
court of Aragon.

J. de Noyon was a prominent minstrel in the court of John I of
Aragon, where he is known to have served in 1378-9.

Jacomi Senleches, known for six lyric pieces, probably hailed from

Pas-de-Calais and was without any doubt in the service of the court of Aragon about 1378; he was also at the court of Castile, where he lamented the death of Eleanor d'Aragon in 1382. He seems to have been an expert performer on the harp.

Grimace, known for five lyric pieces, was probably one of the older generation, contemporary with Machaut but working in the southern courts.

Trebor was yet another poet-musician in the service of John I of Aragon and is known for six or seven lyric compositions.

P. des Molins

⊁26⊁

ballade

De ce que fol pensé souvent remaynt,
Helas, je le puis bien par moy prouver,
3 Car par penser et cuydier me destraint
Amours le corps et fayt mon cuer crever.
5 Ensy m'estuet les griefs maulz endurer
Celéement pour vous, dame honourée,
D'ainsy languir en estrange contrée.

8 Autre bien n'ay, n'autre bien en moy maynt
Fors Souvenir, doulce dame sanz per,
10 Qui me mordrist et mon povre vis taint;
Ce n'est Desir qui m'a fayt comander
12 Qu'Espoir en riens ne me voelle aviser
Par paöur de longue demourée
D'ainsy languir en estrange contrée.

15 Mais, sur ma foy, dame que mon cuer craint
Et que je voeille sur toutes honnourer,
17 Si durement mon las cüer complaint,
Y n'en puet mais, car il ne puet durer
19 Sans vëoir vo tres doulz vïaire cler;
Mais grant joie ay, dame, si vous agrée,
D'ainsy languir en estrange contrée.

40

Magister Franciscus

⊁ 27 ⊁

ballade

Phiton, Phiton, beste tres veneneuse,
Corps terestrin, combien regneras tu?
3 Nés et créés de gent tres haÿneuse,
Prochainement convient que soyés batu
5   De par Phébus le tres bel
Qui siet en haut au gent corps tres isnel,
Qui durement convient que te confonde,
Tu qui contens gaster la flour du monde.

9 Bien te descript Ovide, si crueuse,
Car en venin est toute ta vertu,
11 N'onques ne crut autre si damageuse;
Et se Nature n'eust bien pourveü,
13   Ton esperit plein de fel
Contre le ciel eut fait tel appel
Que de toy produire fust quarte et monde,
Tu qui contens gaster la flour du monde.

17 Et se longtans Fortune tenebreuse
Te sueffre en haut, nïent mains je conclu
19 Que ta durer ne sera pas joyeuse.
Ainsy Phiton ne fu mie abatu
21   D'un tout seul dart sus la pel;
Le tien pour vray que ton cuer si revel
Sera enclos en misere parfonde,
Tu qui contens gaster la flour du monde.

J. Cuvelier

⇥ 28 ⇤

ballade

Se Galäas et le puissant Artus,
Samson le fort, Tristain, Ogier n'Amon
3 De hardement et prouesse cremus,
Prisié, doubté furent et de grant non,
5 Dont doit on bien le noble et haut baron
Doubter, prisier, portans en sa devise:
'*Fébus avant*' *par prouesse conquise.*

8 Car en luÿ ce designe Fébus:
Force, pöoir et dominacïon,
10 Et par avant de chascun est tenus
Prous et hardis, courageus com lïon.
12 Nuls caut contre luÿ lievé penon,
Car en armes porte qui bien l'avise:
'*Fébus avant*' *par prouesse conquise.*

15 De haulte honour et de nobles vertus,
De sens, avis, de largaiche et raison
17 Est adornés, de che ne doubte nus.
La fame enqueurt en mainte regïon;
19 Par les lettres rouges saras le non
De luy disant, à tous vous en avise:
'*Fébus avant*' *par prouesse conquise.*

Philipoctus de Caserta

✦ 29 ✦

ballade

Par le grant senz d'Adriane la sage
Fu Theseüs gardés de perillier
3 Quant à son tour li convient le voyage
En la maison Dedalus essaier.
5 Puis la trahi et la vost essillier;
Fortrait li a un jouel de grant pris
Qu'avoir ne puet sanz O couvert de LIS.

8 Adriane est si noble de linage
Et si puissant c'on la puet raconter;
10 Le jouel ot de son propre heritage
Que Theseüs s'efforsa d'usurper;
12 Et pour l'avoir le tienent en grant dangier.
Se secours n'a, le jouel est peris
Qu'avoir ne puet sanz O couvert de LIS.

15 Mais le lis est de si tres haut parage,
Bel à vëoir, plaisant à manïer,
17 Riche en povoir, de si perfait courage
Qu'à la dame puet sa vertu envier.
19 Rollant ne Hector ne li faut souhaidier
Pour secourir le jouel de grant pris
Qu'avoir ne puet sanz O couvert de LIS.

J. de Noyon

⊁{ 30 }⊬

ballade

Puisque je sui fumeux plains de fumée
Fumer m'estuet, car se je ne fumoye
3 Ceulz qui dïent que j'ay ceste fumée,
Par fumée je les desmentiroye.
5 Et nepourquant jamais ne fumeroye
De fumer qui fust contre raÿson;
Se je fume, c'est ma compleccïon
Quolerique qu'ainsi me fayt fumer.
Je fumeray sanz personne grever;
C'est bien fumé, y n'i a point d'outrayge
Quant on fume sans fayre autruy damage.

12 Fumée n'est à nulli refusée;
Fume qui veult, tenir ne m'en porroie.
14 J'ay en fumant mainte chose fit rimée,
Encore sçay que maïs n'i avenroye
16 Se par fumer en fumant n'i pensoye.
Fumée rent bien consolacïon
Aucune fois tost tribulacïon;
On se puet bien en fumant deliter,
Home fumeux puet en fumant mover
Et si pluseurs profit et avantage
Quant on fume sans fayre autruy damage

23 Se j'eusse la cervellë empeinée
De Socratés si comme je vodroye,
25 J'eusse bien la teste plus temperée,
Car onques ne fuma par nulle voye.
27 Chascuns n'est pas clavis de telle corroye,
Car tel fume que peu s'en parçoyt on;
Tant a du cuer plus de confusïon
Quant i ne puet sa fumée monstrer,
Ou il n'ose pour päour d'enpirer.
Je ne tieng pas c'on ayt le cuer volage
Quant on fume sans fayre autruy damage.

J. Senleches

⋊ 31 ⋉

ballade
Fuions de ci, helas, povre compaigne!
Chascuns s'en voist querir son aventure
3 En Aragon, en France ou en Bretaingne,
Car en brief temps on n'ara de nous cure.
5 Fuions querir no vie non seüre,
Ne demorons yci eure ne jour
Puisque perdu avons Alïenor.

8 Car c'est bien drois, rayson le nous einseigne,
Puisque la Mort tres cruel et obscure
10 Nous a osté la royone d'Espaingne,
Nostre maestresse, no confort et masure;
12 Que chascuns ovre leur volunté pure
De bien briefment vuidier de ce contour
Puisque perdu avons Alïenor.

15 Mais au partir personne ne se faingne
Que de bon cuer et loialté seüre,
17 Ne prie Dieux que l'ame de li preinge
Et qu'elle n'ait sa penitence dure
19 Mais Paradis qui de jour en jour dure.
Et puis pensons d'aler sans nul sejour
Puisque perdu avons Alïenor.

Anonymous

⊰ 32 ⊱

rondeau

Passerose de biauté pure et fine
2 *Et de bonté tres douche flour de lys,*
3 En vous penser tous jours mes cuers ne fine,
4 *Passerose de biauté pure et fine.*
5 Ne quier que altrement ma vie decline,
6 Car sans vous n'ay bien, joye ne delys;
7 *Passerose de biauté pure et fine*
8 *Et de bonté tres douche flour de lys.*

Anonymous

⊰ 33 ⊱

rondeau

En tes doulz flans plains de virginité
2 *Et de excellence plus qu'on ne poroit dire,*
3 Virgene pucelle, portas l'umanité
4 *En tes doulz flans plains de virginité.*
5 Bien doit loër chascuns ta dignité
6 Quant en toi voloit herbergë eslire;
7 *En tes doulz flans plains de virginité*
8 *Et de excellence plus qu'on ne poroit dire.*

Grimace

✠ 34 ✠

virelai

Alarme, alarme, sans sejour
Et sans demour,
Car mon las cuer si est en plour.
Alarme, tost doulce figure,
Alarme, car navrés
Suis de tel pointure
Que mors suy sans nul retour;
Diex en ait l'ame.

9 Si vous suppli, nette et pure,
Pour qui tant de mal endure
Que armer vous voeilliés pour moy
12 Contre ma dolour obscure
Qui me tient en grief ardure
Dont souvent ploure en requoy.

15 Wacarme, wacarme, quel dolour
Et quel langour
Suefre, dame, pour votre amour.
Wacarme, douce creature,
Wacarme, ne me larez
En tel aventure
De mourir en grief tristor
Sans confort d'ame.

23 *Alarme, alarme, sans sejour*
Et sans demour,
Car mon las cuer si est en plour.
Alarme, tost doulce figure,
Alarme, car navrés
Suis de tel pointure
Que mors suy sans nul retour;
Diex en ait l'ame.

Trebor

⊀ 35 ⊁

virelai

Hé, tres doulz roussignol joly
Qui dit occy, occy, occy,
Je te deprie
Que sans detry
Voisses à ma dame jolie
Et dy de par moy et affye
Que ocy, ocy, ocy
M'a se son dur cuer n'amoulie.

9   Alouete qui vas volant
     Si haut et si cler chantant
       Douce chançon,
       Lire, lire, liron
      Tu vas tout voletant,
14 A ma dame seras errant.
      Or li va tantost disant
       Par ma chançon:
       Lire, lire, liron
      Que mon cuer va sentant.

19 Hé, dame, puisqu'il est ainsy
      Qu'en vo merci, merci, merci
        Ay mis ma vie,
        Je vous suplie
      De mon povre cuer que m'en die
      Que tenés en vostre baillie
       Que merci, merci, merci;
      Ayés mercy, par vostre aÿe.

27 *Hé, tres doulz roussignol joly*
Qui dit occy, occy, occy,
  Je te deprie
  Que sans detry
Voisses à ma dame jolie
Et dy de par moy et affye
  Que ocy, ocy, ocy
M'a se son dur cuer n'amoulie.

JEHAN FROISSART

Born in Valenciennes in 1337, Froissart knew the protection of many distinguished patrons including the houses of Brabant and Hainaut, and travelled very widely both in Britain and on the continent. Following a last visit to England he died in oblivion about 1400. Froissart is celebrated above all as a brilliant chronicler of his troubled times, but he also produced a lengthy romance, *Meliador* (which contains a number of lyric pieces composed by his patron Wenceslas of Bohemia), several narrative poems of which some contain lyric pieces of Froissart's own composition (e.g. *Le Paradys d'Amour, L'Espinette amoureuse, La Prison amoureuse, Le joli Buisson de Jonece, Le joli Mois de May, Le Livre du Tresor amoureux*) and a large output of further lyric pieces, though none of them were set to music. Especially interesting is his experimental cross between ballade and rondeau form of which there are thirty-six examples in *Le Livre du Tresor amoureux*.

⊀ 36 ⊁

ballade

Ne quier vëoir Medée ne Jason,
Ne trop avant lire en son mapemonde,
3   Ne la musique Orpheüs ne le son,
Ne Herculès, qui cercha tout le monde,
5   Ne Lucresse, qui tant fu bonne et monde,
Ne Penelope aussi, car, par saint Jame,
Je voi assés, puisque je voi ma dame.

8   Ne quier vëoir Vregile ne Caton,
Ne par quel art orent si grant faconde,
10   Ne Léander, qui tout sans naviron
Nöoit en mer, qui rade est et parfonde,
12   Tout pour l'amour de sa dame la blonde,
Ne nuls rubis, saphir, perle ne jame:
Je voi assés, puisque je voi ma dame.

15 Ne quier vëoir le cheval Pegason,
Qui plus tost court en l'air ne vole aronde,
17 Ne l'image que fist Pymalïon,
Qui n'ot pareil premiere ne seconde,
19 Ne Oleüs, qui en mer boute l'onde;
S'on voet sçavoir pour quoi? Pour ce, par m'ame:
Je voi assés, puisque je voi ma dame.

⊁ 37 ⊁

ballade

Sus toutes flours tient on la rose à belle,
Et en aprés, je croi, la vïolette;
3 La flour de lys est belle, et la perselle;
La flour de glay est plaisans et parfette;
5 Et li pluisour aiment moult l'anquelie,
Le pyone, le muget, la soussie.
Cascune flour a par li son merite;
Mès je vous di, tant que pour ma partie,
Sus toutes flours j'aime la margherite.

10 Car en tous temps, plueve, gresille ou gelle,
Soit la saisons ou fresque, ou laide, ou nette,
12 Ceste flour est gracïeuse et nouvelle,
Douce, plaisans, blanchete et vermillete;
14 Close est à point, ouverte et espanie;
Ja n'y sera morte në apalie;
Toute bonté est dedens li escripte;
Et pour un tant, quant bien y estudie,
Sus toutes flours j'aime la margherite.

19 Et le douc temps ore se renouvelle
Et esclarcist ceste douce flourette;
21 Et si voi ci sëoir dessus l'asprelle
Deus cuers navrés d'une plaisant sajette,
23 A qui le dieu d'Amours soit en aïe.
Avec euls est Plaisance et Courtoisie
Et Douls Regars qui petit les respite.
Dont c'est raison qu'au chapel faire die:
Sus toutes flours j'aime la margherite.

⊁38⊁

Pour exaucier la haulte et noble estrace,
Es biens d'Amours, dont on ne puet joïr
3 Que ce ne soit par sa benigne grace,
Et aussi pour tous bons cuers esjoïr
5 Qui voulroient en honneur conjoïr
Les fais d'amours et d'armes noblement,
Faire vueil par ces deux poins proprement
De balades aucune quantité
Pour y parler, selon mon sentement,
D'armes, d'amours et de moralité.

11 Or est ainsi que voulentiers trouvasse
La maniere de faire le plaisir
13 Aux amoureux, et que je leur monstrasse
En brief de ce qu'ilz voulroient oïr
15 A leur propos et pour les y tenir.
Et pour tant j'ay chascun commencement
Des balades mis ordenéement
O les refrains, en rieule de clarté,
Pour mieulz trouver et plus legierement
D'armes, d'amours et de moralité

21 Par maniere de table qu'on ne passe
Ce dont on veult aucune fois sentir,
23 Car aus refrains puet on en peu d'espasse
Trouver de ce qu'on veult entretenir
25 Pour les argus qui font à soustenir.
Et pour ces cas, j'ay mis fïablement
Nombre à chascun refrain, pour ablement
Y adviser et pour la verité
Savoir de ce que mon petit cuer sent
D'armes, d'amours et de moralité.

✠ 39 ✠

rondeau-ballade

Comment se doit on maintenir
2 *En servant armes et amours,*
3 S'on veult loyauté soustenir?
4 *Comment se doit on maintenir,*
5 Pour verité entretenir?
6 Dites, qui en savés les tours,
7 *Comment se doit on maintenir*
8 *En servant armes et amours?*

9 — *Comment se doit on maintenir,*
   Qui se veult d'armes approchier
11 Et d'amours qui se veult tenir?
   Il ne leur doit pas reprochier
13 Chose dont il les puist courcier,
   Ains se doit vrais amans tousjours
   Courtoisement humilïer
   En servant armes et amours.

17 S'on veult loyauté soustenir
   En tous estas, sans varïer,
19 On doit en son cuer retenir,
   Que, s'uns homs se veult alïer,
21 Il ne se puet plus fort lïer
   Que par sa bouche; en toutes cours
   Doit on loyal homme prisïer
   En servant armes et amours.

25 — *Pour verité entretenir,*
   Vous desistes au comencier
27 Que, qui veult à honneur venir
   D'armes et d'amours, exaucier
29 Les doit qui s'en veult avancier.
   Dites, qui en savez les tours,
   De quoy se puet on mieulz aidier
   En servant armes et amours?

❧ 40 ❧

On ne pourroit trop loër bon Amour
2 *Au dit de ceulz qui aiment loyaument,*
3 En bien, en paix, en plaisance, en doulçour;
4 *On ne pourroit trop loër bon Amour,*
5 N'on ne saroit esprisier sa valour;
6 Pour ses biens fais essaucier haultement,
7 *On ne pourroit trop loër bon Amour,*
8 *Au dit de ceulz qui aiment loyaument.*

9 *On ne pourroit trop loër bon Amour*
Au dit de ceulz qui sont de sa baniere,
11 Mais, je vous pri, mettez me hors d'errour
Et me dites se plus d'une maniere
13 D'amours se fait bonne, vraie et entiere.
Aucuns dient qu'en amours leur ennoie
Et que leur cuer en lermes font et noye,
Et li aucun s'en loënt grandement.
Ne sçay qu'en est, mais de ce me tenroie
Au dit de ceulz qui aiment loyaument.

19 *En bien, en paix, en plaisance, en doulçour*
Se tient Amours loyal et droituriere,
21 N'onques ne fu en courage d'onnour
De bon Amour estainte la lumiere
23 Que par le fait de varïence fiere,
Car bon Amour en loyauté s'esjoie
Et ne requiert qu'amour, soulas et joie
En tous estas. Qui diroit autrement,
De ce fait cy je m'en reporteroie
Au dit de ceulz qui aiment loyaument.

29 *On ne saroit esprisier sa valour,*
Ne de ses biens l'abundance pleniere,
31 Et pour mettre nostre fait au retour
Que demandé vous ay à lie chiere,
33 S'il est d'amour plus d'une, tant soit chiere,
Car, pour certain, volentiers me rendroie
A la meilleur et m'y obligeroie
Pour ses biens fais essaucier haultement,
Et si croy bien qu'en brief temps le saroie
Au dit de ceulz qui aiment loyaument.

➤{ 41 }➤

rondeau

On se doit souffrir et taire
2 *Et tout en gré recevoir*
Quanqu'Amours ordonne, voir;

4 *Et s'on sent griefté ne haire,*
5 *On se doit souffrir et taire.*

6 Car tous confors poet parfaire
7 Amours par son grant pöoir;
Pour ce di de bon voloir:

9 *On se doit souffrir et taire*
10 *Et tout en gré recevoir*
Quanqu'Amours ordonne, voir.

➤{ 42 }➤

virelai

Moult m'est tart que je revoie
La tres douce, simple et quoie
Que j'aim loyalment
Et pour qui certainnement
Ce sejour m'anoie.

55

6   Lonc temps a que ne le vi
Ne que parler n'en oï,
    S'en vif en tristour,

9   Car, en son maintien joli
Et ou plaisant corps de li,
    Garni de valour,

12   Tous esbatements prendroie,
Et par ensi je vivoie
    Tres joiousement;
Or me fault souffrir tourment
    Ens ou lieu de joie.

17   *Moult m'est tart que je revoie*
La tres douce, simple et quoie,
    Que j'aim loyalment
Et pour qui certainnement
    Ce sejour m'anoie.

22   Amours, dittes li ensi:
Qu'onques amans ne souffri
    Si forte labour

25   Que j'ai souffert pour li ci
Et souffrerai autressi
    Jusqu'à mon retour.

28   C'est raisons qu'elle m'en croie,
Car, quelque part que je voie,
    Tant l'aim ardammant
Il m'est avis vraiement
    Que tout dis le voie.

33   *Moult m'est tart que je revoie*
La tres douce, simple et quoie,
    Que j'aim loyalment
Et pour qui certainnement
    Ce sejour m'anoie.

LE LIVRE DES CENT BALLADES

The idea of writing a collection of exactly one hundred items was popular in the middle ages. Alain Chartier, for instance, follows this procedure in his *La belle dame sans mercy* and Christine de Pisan wrote two groups of a hundred ballades.

The *Livre des cent ballades* was mainly written by Jean, Sénéchal d'Eu, while he was a prisoner in Egypt during a campaign of Philippe d'Artois in 1387–8. The author presents himself as a young squire seeking advice on love; the first fifty ballades give the advice of an older knight, who advocates *loyauté*, and this is countered by the last fifty ballades in which a lady recommends *fausseté*.

On the campaigners' return to France in 1389 the poems were presented in the brilliant entourage of Louis de France, brother of Charles VI; the ensuing debate produced the *Responces des Balades*, composed by a number of the most distinguished personages of the day.

⊀43⊁

ballade

Frere, oÿ m'avez raconter
Une partie des travaulx
3 Qu'Amours fait à ceulx endurer
Qui estre ne veulent loiaux,
5 Mais non pas tous, car tant de maulx
Y a que je n'en sçay le nombre;
Pour ce, vous pry que dessoubz l'ombre
De fausseté ne vous logiez,
Car tous les maulx en arïez
Que dit vous ay, sans nulle faille;
Car Amours veult tousjours paier
Les fausses gens, comment qu'il aille,
De tel service tel loier.

57

14 Ne point n'y fault; pour ce, garder
    Se doit chascun qu'il ne soit faulx;
16 Car qui la vie en veult mener,
    Il ne peut que les durs assaulx
18 De faulseté la desloiaux
    Ne viengnent en lui sans semondre,
    Tant qu'en douleur là faille fondre;
    Ne remede n'y sariez
    Mettre, se venus estïez
    A ce point là nommé, tant vaille;
    Car nul ne peut contralïer
    Vers Amours, qu'en fin ne lui baille
    De tel service tel loier.

27 Ainsi veult Amours ordonner
    Ses nobles jugemens royaulx.
29 Par faulseté fait tourmenter
    Ceulx qui sont si desnaturaulx
31 Qu'à ses euvres sont communaulx;
    Sans menacier, sy les encombre
    Qu'on les pourroit lïer et tondre;
    Quant en ses laz sont trebuchiez,
    Jamais n'en seront deslïez;
    Là les estraint, point et travaille,
    En faisant de vie dangier.
    Ainsi leur paie, compte et taille
    De tel service tel loier.

⚜ 44 ⚜

Sy prions tous les amoureux
    Que chascun seulz
Par une balade savoir
4 Nous face lequel des conseulx
    Leur semble entr'eulx
Mieudre à tenir, à dire voir:
7 Qui cuer d'amant fait moins doloir,
    Qui plus povoir
Lui donne de devenir preux,
Qui plus plaisans biens recevoir
    Fait et avoir,
Qui plus le fait d'Amours joieux.

13 Les argumens sont merveilleux,
    Et poy pareulx;
Mais chascun cuide parcevoir
16 Son conseil estre gracïeux
    Et revelleux
Plus que l'autre, et trop mieux valoir.
19 Sy faisons, pour paix pourcevoir,
    Nostre devoir
De l'enquerre, sans estre oiseux.
Or die chascun son vouloir,
    Sans decevoir,
Qui plus le fait d'Amours joieux.

25 Et que chascun soit desireux
Et curïeux
De tous ces points ramentevoir,
28 Et lise les debas des deux,
Car dangereuz
Est leur propos à concevoir.
31 Sy nous veulliez faire vëoir
Et apparoir,
Par vo dit, le plus eüreux
Conseil dont amant, main et soir,
Peut miex sçavoir
Qui plus le fait d'Amours joieux.

(Monseigneur Le Duc De Berry)

⊁45⊁

ballade

Puiz qu'à Amours suis si gras eschappé
Que moult petit me pevent jamais nuire,
3 Parle qui veult, je suis reconforté,
S'aucun vouloit pour ce de moy mesdire.
5 Mais du debat mon oppinïon dire
Veul à tous ceulx qui la voudront oïr.
L'un de vous dit qu'on doit son bien querir
Au premier prest, l'autre dit du contraire;
Mais mon aviz, qui s'i voudra tenir,
On peut l'un dire et l'autre doit on faire.

11 Dire qu'on veult seulement loiauté
Et que c'est droit que tout cuer s'i atire,
13 Mais du faire n'aiez ja volenté,
Tendez tousdis à la fin qu'on desire;
15 Ne vous chaille s'on vous veult escondire;
Alez ailleurs, pensez de parfournir.
Esploittiez fort, laissez en convenir
A plaisance qui veult à chascun plaire;
Car, qui s'i veult sagement contenir,
On peut l'un dire et l'autre doit on faire.

21 Pour ce je tien à trop mal conseillié
   Cellui qui veult seule maistresse eslire,
23 Et li plusieurs se treuvent courroucié
   D'avoir usé leur temps en tel martire;
25 Car de leur deuil se scevent moult bien rire
   Celles meismes qu'ilz tant veulent cherir.
   Mieux leur vausist partout Dame choisir,
   Non pas une, mais trois ou quatre paire,
   Et à toutes, pour leur grace acquérir,
   On peut l'un dire et l'autre doit on faire.

EUSTACHE DESCHAMPS

Eustache Deschamps was possibly Machaut's nephew and certainly admired him greatly, though none of his own considerable output of lyric verse (1,017 ballades, 171 rondeaux, 84 virelais, 139 chansons royales, 14 lais) is set to music.

Born in 1346, Deschamps studied at the University of Orléans and spent much of his life in the service of Philippe, duc d'Orléans, later, of Louis, duc d'Orléans, brother of Charles VI, and, indeed, in the service of the king himself. When he died in 1406 Deschamps, who travelled widely, had witnessed over fifty years of troubled events and seen four generations of French kings pass by. The ballades in particular reflect Deschamps' desire to be a chronicler of his times in verse, a refreshing contrast to the bulk of courtly poetry, and also give us clear insight into the poet's own very individual character.

Deschamps' *Art de Dictier,* written in 1392, is important for the rules it gives for the composition of lyric forms and for the distinction it makes between 'natural music' (i.e. poetry) and 'artificial music' (i.e. music) as well as for its position as the first in a tradition of treatises on versification in French.

⋆⊰ 46 ⊱⋆

ballade

J'ay mes livres en tant de lieux prestez
Et à pluseurs qui les devoient rendre,
3 Dont li termes est failliz et passez,
Qu'à faire prest ne doy jamès entendre,
5 Laiz, ne chançons, ne faiz d'amours comprandre,
Ystorier, n'oneur ramentevoir;
Quant je me voy sanz cause decevoir,
Et retenir mon labeur et ma paine,
Dolens en sui, à Dieu jure, pour voir,
Plus ne prestray livre quoy qui aviengne.

11   Il souffist bien que je soie entestez,
     Que j'aie mis mon labeur en apprandre,
13   Et se j'ay fait en mes chetivetez
     Chose qui soit où biens se doye prandre,
15   Donner le vueil lïement, non pas vendre,
     Mais qu'on face de l'escripre devoir
     En mon hostel; pour ce, à tous faiz sçavoir
     Que desormais nulz requerir n'ampraigne
     De mes livres ne mes papiers avoir:
     Plus ne prestray livre quoy qui aviengne.

21   Perdu en ai maint, dont je suis troublez,
     Par emprunter, et ce me fait deffendre
23   Que jamais nul ne m'en sera ostez
     Par tel moien, à quoy nul ne doit tendre.
25   De ce serment ne me doit nulz reprandre,
     Mais qui vouldra de mes choses sçavoir,
     Très voulentiers l'en feray apparoir,
     Sanz porter hors; vëoir vers moi les viengne,
     Se sires n'est qui ait trop grant povoir:
     Plus ne prestray livre quoy qui aviengne.

l'envoy

31   Prince, Eustaces, qui a la teste tendre,
     Supplie à tous que dés or leur souviengne
     De mes livres non retenir, n'emprandre:
     Plus ne prestray livre quoy qui aviengne.

⨀ 47 ⨀

ballade

     Dont viens tu ? — De vëoir m'amie.
      — Qu'i as tu fait? — Tout mon plesir.
3   — L'aimes tu bien? — N'en doubtez mie.
      — T'aime elle fort? — Jusqu'au mourir.
5   — Que scez tu? — Que veu l'ay souffrir
     Tant comme on puet pour son amant
     De mal, d'anuy, de desplaisir.
     — Or soit il pendus qui en ment.

9 — Ainsi soit il; je ne mens mye.
— Harou! tu me faiz esbahir.
11 — Pourquoy? — Car pas n'ay d'ademie.
Telle amour trop me fait d'aïr:
13 En lieu d'amer me veult haïr
Celle que j'aime loyaument;
D'elle ne puis à chief venir.
— *Or soit il pendus qui en ment.*

17 — Pas ne mens, je te certiffie.
— Dont ne sés tu pas bien servir?
19 — Sy faiz, maiz po en moy se fye;
Tousjours dit que la viel trahir,
21 Et pour ce ne l'ose envahir.
— Tu es folz, poursui hardiment.
— Voyre, maiz autre en voy joïr!
— *Or soit il pendus qui en ment.*

l'envoy

25 Princes, qui n'ayme c'est folie,
Maiz qu'il sache mentir souvent.
On en vault mieulx aucune fye;
Or soit il pendus qui en ment.

⇥ 48 ⇤

ballade En dimenche, le tiers jour de decembre,
L'an mil .ccc. avec soixante et huit,
3 Fut a Saint Pol nex dedenz une chambre
Charles li Roys, .iii. heures puis minuit,
5 Filz de Charles, cinquiesme de ce nom,
Roy des François, de Jehanne de Bourbon,
Roine à ce temps couronnée de France,
Le premier jour de l'Advent qui fut bon;
Par ce sçara chascune ceste naissance.

10 Ou signe estoit, si comme je me membre,
De la vierge la lune en celle nuit,
12 En la face seconde; et si remembre
Qu'au sixte jour dudit mois fut conduit
14 Et baptizié à Saint Pol, ce scet on,
Ou il avoit maint prince et maint baron:
Montmorancy, Dampmartin sanz doubtance.
Tous deux Charles leverent l'enfançon:
Par ce sçara chascune ceste naissance.

19 Trois ans aprés quant li mois de mars entre
A treize jour, sabmedi, saichent tuit,
21 L'an mil .ccc. .lx. et onze, entendre
Puet un chascun la naissance et le bruit
23 De Loÿs né, frere du Roy Charlon,
Après mie nuit trois heures environ;
La lune estoit à .ix. jours de croissance;
Marraine fut madame d'Alençon:
Par ce sçara chascune ceste naissance.

l'envoy
28 Princes, parrains fut Bertran, li prodom
Connestables, qui tant ot de renom,
De vostre frere; aiez en souvenance:
A Saint Pol fut nez en vostre maison,
Et baptisiez fut par Jehan de Craon:
Par ce sçara chascune ceste naissance.

⊹{ 49 }⊹

A vous, monseigneur d'Orliens,
Treshumblement supplie Eustache
3 Que comme il soit des ancïens
Voz serviteurs par longue espace
5 De temps, que de vostre humble grace,
Attendu la debilité
De son chief et fragilité,
Son estat, sa povre nature,
Qu'il ait par vostre autorité
Chaperon tant comme yver dure,

11 Sanz deffubler, car il n'est riens
Qui tant de mal en corps li face,
13 Ce dient les phisicïens,
Que le froit qui par son chief glace
15 En son estomac froit com glace,
Et lors a en duplicité
Toux et reume en tel quantité
Que c'est du raconter laidure.
Or ait donc par vostre pité
Chaperon tant comme yver dure,

21 Ou venir n'osera cïens
Jusqu'à ce que l'yver se passe,
23 Car du chief est si pacïens
A present qu'à paine en respasse;
25 Et cilz est trop foulz qui trespasse
Et muert de froit par voulenté,
Et qui ne garde sa santé,
Car mort craint toute creature.
Ait Eustache par vo bonté
Chaperon tant comme yver dure.

l'envoy

31   Princes, la povre humanité
    Pour honeur ne pour vanité
    Qui ne lui vault, n'ait de ce cure
    Puis qu'autre en ait debilité;
    Laissiez moy par humilité
    Chaperon tant comme yver dure.

⊁ 50 & 51 ⊁

double ballade   Armes, Amours, Dames, Chevalerie,
    Clers, musicans et fayseurs en françoys,
3   Tous soffistes et toute poetrie,
    Tous cheus qui ont melodieuses vois,
5   Ceus qui chantent en orgue aucunes foys
    Et qui ont cher le doulz art de musique,
    Demenés duel, plourés, car c'est bien drois,
    La mort Machaut le noble rethouryque.

9   Onques d'amours ne parla en follie,
    Ains a esté en tous ses dis courtois;
11 Aussi a moult pleü sa chanterie
    As grans seigneurs, aus contes, aus bourgois.
13 Hé, Horpheüs! assés lamenter te dois
    Et regreter d'un regret autentique,
    Artheüs aussy, Alpheüs tous trois,
    La mort Machaut le noble rethouryque.

17 Priés pour li siques nuls ne l'oublie,
    Ce vous requiert le bailli de Valois,
19 Car il n'est aujord'uy nul en vie
    Tel com il fut, ne ne sera des moys;
21 Complains sera de contes et de roys
    Jusqu'à lonc temps pour sa bone practique;
    Vestés vous de noir, plourés tous, Champenois,
    La mort Machaut le noble rethouryque.

⁘ ⁘ ⁘

O flour des flours de toute melodie,
Tres doulz maistres qui tant fuestes adrois,
3 Guillaume, mondains diex d'armonie,
Après vos fais, qui obtendra le choys
5 Sur tous fayseurs? Certes, ne le congnoys.
Vo nom sera precïeuse relique,
Car l'on ploura en France et en Artois
La mort Machaut le noble rethouryque.

9 Le fons chierie et la fontayne helie
Dont vous estes le ruissel et le dois
11 Où poetes mirent leur estudie,
Convient taire, dont je suis molt destrois.
13 Las! c'est pour vous qui mort gisiés tous frois,
Ay mi! dolent departit faillant replique;
Plourés arples et cors saracynois
La mort Machaut le noble rethouryque.

17 Plourés rebebe, viele et ciphonie,
Psalterïon, tous instrumens courtois,
19 Guisternes, fleustes, herpes et chelemie
Et traversaynes et vous, nymphes de bois;
21 Timpane aussi, metés onnour, se doys
Tous instrumens qui estes tout antique;
Faites devoir, plourés, gentil Galoys,
La mort Machaut le noble rethouryque.

⚜52⚜

ballade
Aprés Machaut qui tant vous a amé
Et qui estoit la fleur de toutes flours,
3 Noble pöete et faiseur renommé,
Plus qu'Ovide vray remede d'amours,
5 Qui m'a nourry et fait maintes douçours,
Veuillés, lui mort, pour l'onneur de celui,
Que je soie vostre loyal ami.

8 Tous instrumens l'ont complaint et plouré:
Musique a fait son obseque et ses plours,
10 Et Orpheüs a le corps enterré
Qui, pour sa mort, est emmutys et sours;
12 Ses tresdoulx chans sont muëz en doulours.
Autel de moy, s'ainsi n'est quant à my
Que je soie vostre loyal ami.

15 Eustace suis par droit nom appellé.
Hé! Peronne, qui estes mes recours,
17 Qui en tous cas bien faictes à mon gré,
Je vous pry que vous me faictes secours:
19 En recevant mes piteuses clamours
Me recréez, s'il vous plairä ainsi
Que je soie vostre loyal ami.

⊀53⊱

ballade

Ceuls qui ne partent de l'ostel
Sanz aler en divers païs,
3 Ne scevent la dolour mortel
Dont gens qui vont sont envahis,
5 Les maulx, les doubtes, les perilz
Des mers, des fleuves et des pas,
Les langaiges qu'om n'entent pas,
La paine et le traveil des corps;
Mais combien qu'om soit de ce las,
Il ne scet rien qui ne va hors.

69

11 Car par le monde universel
Qui est des nobles poursuïs,
13 Sont choses à chascun costel
Dont maint seroient esbahis,
15 De la créance, des habis,
Des vivres, des divers estas,
Des bestes, des merveilleux cas,
Des poissons, oiseaulx, serpens fors,
Des roches, des plains, des lieux bas:
Il ne scet rien qui ne va hors.

21 De vir les montaignes de sel,
Les baings chaux dont maint sont garis,
23 Le cours desquelz est naturel
Par vaines de soufre tramis,
25 Les divers fruits, ermines, gris;
Minieres d'or, d'argent à tas,
De fer, d'acier, d'estain verras,
De plomb, cuivre, arrain, et alors
A toutes gens dire pourras:
Il ne scet rien qui ne va hors.

l'envoy

31 Princes, nulz ne sera sutils,
Saiges, courtois ne bien apris,
Tant soit riches, puissans ou fors,
S'en divers voyages n'est mis
En jeunesce pour avoir pris;
Il ne scet rien qui ne va hors.

⊁54⊁

ballade

Age de plomb, temps pervers, ciel d'arain,
Terre sanz fruit, et sterile et brehaingne,
3 Peuple maudit de toute doleur plain,
Il est bien drois que de vous tous me plaingne:
5 Car je ne voy riens au monde qui viengne
Fors tristement et à confusïon,
Et qui tous maulx en ses faiz ne compraingne,
Hui est li temps de tribulacïon.

9 C'est par pechié, de ce soion certain,
Qui nous emfle plus que venin l'yraigne;
11 De Dieu servir sommes recuit et vain,
Et d'obeir à ce qu'il nous enseigne.
13 Et pour ce vient toute guerre mondaine,
Faulte de biens, mort, persecucïon
Qui nous destruit; d'ajuder nous souviengne:
Hui est li temps de tribulacïon.

17 Et si n'avons point d'ui ne de demain,
Que li pechiez et la mort ne nous praingne
19 En un moment et par un cas soudain,
Et si n'est nul qui du mal se restraingne;
21 Or y pensons, car ja droitte est l'enseigne
Et li glaives de no pugnicïon:
Crions mercy, qu'emfers ne nous souspraingne,
Hui est li temps de tribulacïon.

⊁55⊁

ballade

Je vueil cesser mon livre de memoire
Ou j'ay escript depuis .xxxii. ans
3   Du saige roy Charle le quint l'istoire,
Les prouesces que fist li bons Bertrans,
5   Connestable de Guesclin, qui engrans
Fut de garder l'utilité publique,
Et qui maintint si sa guerre punique
Sur les Anglois, que France reformée
En fut et est par mainte belle armée
Faitte à son temps, et mourut en la guerre
De son segnour; moult fut sa mort plourée:
Noble chose est de bon renom acquerre!

13   Car quant sa mort fut au bon roy notoire,
Moult fut ses duelz et sa complainte grans
15   D'avoir perdu le prince de victoire;
Pour son peuplë et païs fut dolens.
17   Lors en souspirs et en larmes plourans,
Dieu mercia, et service autentique
Fist pour la mort du bon prodomme, si que
A Saint Denis fut la tombe ordonnée,
Parfaicte non, mainte aumosne donnée
Pour son salut par devers Dieu acquerre;
Des trois mestiers fut l'ofrande portée:
Noble chose est de bon renom acquerre!

25 Brief temps aprés, de ceste vie engloire
    Passa ly rois qui laissa deux enfans,
27 Charle et Loÿs, mais nulz ne pourroit croire
    Les grans meschiez qu'eurent les mendres d'ans,
29 Rebellions de leur peuple et contens,
    En bail cheirent, le temps fut lors inique.
    Charles regna, à Reims prist sa laurique;
    La chose fut assez bien gouvernée.
    Puis son sacre me fut paine donnée
    Estans o eulx, d'encerchier et enquerre
    Et d'escripre leurs faiz par la contrée:
    Noble chose est de bon renom acquerre!

≺56≻

ballade

Qui veult son corps en santé maintenir
    Et resister à mort d'epidemie,
3 Il doit courroux et tristece fuir,
    Laissier le lieu ou est la maladie
5 Et frequenter joieuse compaignie,
    Boire bon vin, nette viande user,
    Port bonne odour contre la punaisie,
    Et ne voist hors s'il ne fait bel et cler.

9 Jeun estomac ne se doit point partir,
    Boire matin et mener sobre vie,
11 Face cler feu en sa chambre tenir;
    De femme avoir ne li souviengne mie;
13 Bains, estuves à son povoir devie,
    Car les humeurs font mouvoir et troubler;
    Soit bien vestus, ait toudis chiere lie,
    Et ne voist hors s'il ne fait bel et cler.

17 De grosses chars et de choulz abstenir
   Et de tous fruiz se doit on en partie,
19 Cler vin avoir, sa poulaille rostie,
   Connins, perdriz, et pour espicerie
21 Canelle avoir, safrain, gingembre, et prie
   Tout d'aigrevin et vergus destremper,
   Dormir au main; ce regime n'oublie,
   Et ne voist hors s'il ne fait bel et cler.

⚜ 57 ⚜

ballade

Muse eloquent entre les .ix., Christine,
Nompareille que je saiche au jour d'ui,
3 En sens acquis et en toute dotrine,
  Tu as de Dieu science et non d'autruy;
5 Tes epistres et livres, que je luy
  En plusieurs lieux, de grant philosophie,
  Et ce que tu m'as escript une fie,
  Me font certain de la grant habondance
  De ton sçavoir qui tousjours monteplie,
  Seule en tes faiz ou royaume de France.

11 Dieu t'a donné de Salemon le signe,
   Cuer ensaignant qu'il demanda de lui;
13 A l'estude es, ou tu ensuis la ligne
   Du bon maistre Thomas, que je congnuy,
15 De Boulongne, Pizain, recors en suy:
   Ton pere fut docteur d'astronomie;
   Charles le Quint, roy, ne l'oublia mie,
   Mais le manda pour sa grant souffisance,
   Et tu l'ensuis és .vii. ars de clergie,
   Seule en tes faiz ou royaume de France.

21 Ha! quelle honeur entre les femmes digne
   Et les hommes? Pour aprandre à toy fuy,
23 Qui trop te plains de la fausse racine
   Dont le fruit fait à tout le monde ennuy;
25 Par t'espitre le voy, que je reçuy
   Benignement, dont cent foiz te mercie;
   Mais plus à plain sçaras de ma partie,
   Qui en tous cas te faiz obeissance,
   Le remede de ta grief maladie,
   Seule en tes faiz ou royaume de France.

l'envoy

31 O douce suer, je, Eustace, te prie,
   Comme ton serf, d'estre en ta compaignie
   Pour bien avoir d'estude congnoissance;
   Mieulx en vaudray tous les temps de ma vie,
   Car je te voy, com Böece à Pavie,
   Seule en tes faiz ou royaume de France.

⚜ 58 ⚜

ballade

   Je deviens courbes et bossus,
   J'oy tres dur, ma vie decline,
3 Je pers mes cheveulx par dessus,
   Je flue en chascune narine,
5 J'ay grant doleur en la poitrine,
   Mes membres sens ja tous trembler,
   Je suis treshastis à parler,
   Impaciens, Desdaing me mort,
   Sanz conduit ne sçay mès aler:
   Ce sont les signes de la mort.

11 Couvoiteus suis, blans et chanus,
Eschars, courroceux; j'adevine
13 Ce qui n'est pas, et loë plus
Le temps passé que la dotrine
15 Du temps present; mon corps se mine;
Je voy envix rire et jouer,
J'ay grant plaisir à grumeler,
Car le temps passé me remort;
Tousjours vueil jeunesce blamer:
Ce sont les signes de la mort.

21 Mes dens sont longs, foibles, agus,
Jaunes, flairans comme santine;
23 Tous mes corps est frois devenus,
Maigres et secs; par medecine
25 Vivre me fault; char ne cuisine
Ne puis qu'à grant paine avaler;
Des jeusnes me fault baler,
Mes corps toudis sommeille ou dort,
Et ne vueil que boire et humer:
Ce sont les signes de la mort.

l'envoy

31 Princes, encor vueil cy adjouster
Soixante ans, pour mieulx confermer
Ma viellesce qui me nuit fort,
Quant ceuls qui me doivent amer
Me souhaident ja oultre mer.
Ce sont les signes de la mort.

⤐{ 59 }⤐

chanson royal

Force de corps, qu'est devenu Sanson?
Où est Auglas, le bon practicïen?
Où est le corps du sage Salemon
Ne d'Ypocras, le bon phisicïen?
Où est Platon, le grant naturïen,
Ne Orpheüs o sa doulce musique?
Tholomeüs o son arismetique,
Ne Dedalus qui fist le bel ouvrage?
Ilz sont tous mors, si fu leur mort inique;
Tuit y mourront, et li fol et li saige.

11   Qu'est devenus Denys, le roy felon?
Alixandre, Salhadin, roy paien,
Albumassar? Mort sont, fors que leur nom.
Mathussalé, qui tant fu ancïen,
Virgille aussi, grant astronomïen,
Julles Cesar et sa guerre punique,
Auffricanus Scipïo, qui Auffrique
Pour les Rommains conquist par son bernage?
Redigez sont ceulz en cendre publique;
Tuit y mourront, et li fol et li saige.

21   Où est Artus, Godeffroy de Buillon,
Judith, Hester, Penelope, Arrïen,
Semiramis, le poissant roy Charlon,
George, Denys, Christofle, Julïen,
Pierres et Pols, maint autre crestïen,
Et les martirs? La mort à tous s'applique;
Nulz advocas pour quelconque replique
Ne scet plaidier sanz passer ce passage,
Ne chevalier, tant ait ermine frique;
Tuit y mourront, et li fol et li saige.

77

31 Puisqu'ainsi est, et que n'y avison?
Laisse chascun le mal, face le bien.
A ces princes cy dessus nous miron
Et aux autres qui n'emporterent rien
A leurs trespas fors leurs biens fais, retien,
Pour l'ame d'eulz; leur renom auttentique
N'est qu'à leurs hoirs d'exemple une partie,
D'eulz ressembler en sens, en vasselage;
Ce monde est vain, decourant, erratique;
Tuit y mourront, et li fol et li saige.

41 Mais j'en voy pou qui en deviengne bon
Et qui n'ait chier l'autrui avec le sien;
De convoitise ont banniere et panon
Maint gouverneur de peuple terrïen;
Las! homs mortelz, de tel vice te abstien,
En gouvernant par le droit polletique;
Ce que Dieu dit regarde en Levitique,
Si ne feras jamais pechié n'oultrage.
Preste est la mort pour toy bailler la brique;
Tuit y mourront, et li fol et li saige.

l'envoy

51 Prince mondains, citez, terres, donjon,
Biauté de corps, force, sens, riche don,
Joliveté, ne vostre hault parage,
Ne vous vauldront que Mort de son baston
Ne vous fiere soit à bas ou hault ton;
Tuit y mourront, et li fol et li saige.

78

⊰ 60 ⊱

Sui je, sui je, sui je belle?

2 Il me semble, à mon avis,
3 Que j'ay beau front et doulz viz
4 Et la bouche vermeillette;
5 *Dittes moy se je suis belle.*

6 J'ay vers yeulx, petis sourcis,
   Le chief blont, le nez traitis,

   Ront menton, blanche gorgette;
   Sui je, sui je, sui je belle?

10 J'ay dur sain et hault assis,
    Lons bras, gresles doys aussis

    Et par le faulz sui greslette;
    Dittes moy se je suis belle.

14 J'ay bonnes rains, ce m'est vis,
    Bon dos, bon cul de Paris,

    Cuisses et gambes bien faictes;
    Sui je, sui je, sui je belle?

18 J'ay piez rondes et petiz,
    Bien chaussans, et biaux habis,

    Je sui gaye et joliette;
    Dittes moy se je suis belle.

22 J'ay mantiaux fourrez de gris,
    J'ay chapiaux, j'ay biaux proffis

    Et d'argent mainte espinglette;
    Sui je, sui je, sui je belle?

26 J'ay draps de soye et tabis,
    J'ay draps d'or et blans et bis,

    J'ay mainte bonne chosette;
    Dittes moy se je suis belle.

30 Que .xv. ans n'ay, je vous dis;
  Moult est mes tresors jolys,

  S'en garderay la clavette;
  Sui je, sui je, sui je belle?

34 Bien devra estre hardis
  Cilz qui sera mes amis,

  Qui ara tel damoiselle;
  Dittes moy se je suis belle.

38 Et par Dieu je li plevis
  Que tresloyal, se je vis,

  Li seray, si ne chancelle;
  Sui je, sui je, sui je belle?

42 Se courtois est et gentilz,
  Vaillans aprés, bien apris,

  Il gaignera sa querelle;
  Dittes moy se je suis belle.

CHRISTINE DE PISAN

Christine de Pisan was born in Venice *c.* 1363. Her father Thomas de Pisan, a distinguished philosopher and astrologer, was invited to the court of Charles V of France in 1368; Christine thus grew up in the sophisticated atmosphere of the French court and she married a young Picard gentleman, Etienne du Castel, in 1378. Her happiness was clouded, however, when in 1389 her husband died, leaving her twenty-five years old, a widow with three children. She then turned to writing and study professionally and produced a very varied and extensive output in both verse and prose, circulating a great number of specially copied and illuminated manuscripts of her works in order to acquire patronage and spread her reputation. She died about 1431.

In lyric verse she produced, apart from her own *Cent Ballades* and *Cent Ballades d'Amant et de Dame,* about a hundred further ballades, twenty virelais, sixty-nine rondeaux, two lais and other works such as the *Livre du duc des vrais amans* into which lyric pieces are inserted. Christine de Pisan treats a diversity of subjects in her poems and on occasion reveals a deeply personal inspiration. Technically she displays an experimental approach, elaborating the traditional forms, now completely free from the dictates of musical considerations, and especially exploits the shortened refrain in the Rondeau.

⇥61⇤

ballade

Doulce chosë est que mariage,
Je le puis bien par moy prouver,
3 Voire à qui mari bon et sage
A, comme Dieu m'a fait trouver.
5 Louez en soit il qui sauver
Le me vueille, car son grant bien
De fait je puis bien esprouver,
Et certes le doulz m'aime bien.

9 La premiere nuit du mariage
Treslors poz je bien esprouver
11 Son grant bien, car oncques oultrage
Ne me fist, dont me deust grever,
13 Mais, ains qu'il fust temps de lever,
Cent fois baisa, si com je tien,
Sanz villennie autre rouver,
Et certes le doulz m'aime bien.

17 Et disoit, par si doulz langage;
'Dieux m'a fait à vous arriver,
19 Doulce amie, et pour vostre usage
Je croy qu'il me fist eslever.'
21 Ainsi ne fina de resver
Toute nuit en si fait maintien
Sanz autrement soy desriver,
Et certes le doulz m'aime bien.

l'envoy

25 Princes, d'amours me fait desver
Quant il me dit qu'il est tout mien;
De doulçour me fera crever,
Et certes le doulz m'aime bien.

⇥ 62 ⇤

ballade Dueil engoisseux, rage desmesurée,
Grief desespoir, plein de forsennement,
3 Langour sanz fin, vie maleürée
Pleine de plour, d'engoisse et de tourment,
5 Cuer doloreux qui vit obscurement,
Tenebreux corps sus le point de perir,
Ay, sanz cesser, continuellement;
Et si ne puis ne garir ne morir.

9 Fierté, durté de joye separée,
Triste penser, parfont gemissement,
11 Engoisse grant en las cuer enserrée,
Courroux amer porté couvertement,
13 Morne maintien sanz resjoïssement,
Espoir dolent qui tous biens fait tarir,
Si sont en moy, sanz partir nullement;
Et si ne puis ne garir ne morir.

17 Soussi, anuy qui tous jours a durée,
Aspre veillier, tressaillir en dorment,
19 Labour en vain, à chiere alangourée
En grief travail infortunéement,
21 Et tout le mal, qu'on puet entierement
Dire et penser sanz espoir de garir,
Me tourmentent desmesuréement;
Et si ne puis ne garir ne morir.

l'envoy

25 Princes, priez à Dieu qui bien briefment
Me doint la mort, s'autrement secourir
Ne veult le mal ou languis durement;
Et si ne puis ne garir ne morir.

⤜ 63 ⤛

ballade

Seulete suy et seulete vueil estre,
Seulete m'a mon doulz ami laissiée,
3 Seulete suy, sanz compaignon ne maistre,
Seulete suy, dolente et courrouciée,
5 Seulete suy en languour mesaisiée,
Seulete suy plus que nulle esgarée,
Seulete suy sanz ami demourée.

8 Seulete suy à huis ou à fenestre,
Seulete suy en un anglet muciée,
10 Seulete suy pour moy de plours repaistre,
Seulete suy, dolente ou apaisiée,
12 Seulete suy, riens n'est qui tant me siée,
Seulete suy en ma chambre enserrée,
Seulete suy sanz ami demourée.

15 Seulete suy partout et en tout estre.
Seulete suy, ou je voise ou je siée,
17 Seulete suy plus qu'autre riens terrestre,
Seulete suy de chascun delaissiée,
19 Seulete suy durement abaissiée,
Seulete suy souvent toute esplourée,
Seulete suy sanz ami demourée.

l'envoy

22 Princes, or est ma doulour commenciée:
Seulete suy de tout dueil menaciée,
Seulete suy plus tainte que morée,
Seulete suy sanz ami demourée.

⇥64⇤

ballade

Que ferons nous de ce mary jaloux?
Je pry à Dieu qu'on le puist escorchier.
3 Tant se prent il de près garde de nous
Que ne povons l'un de l'autre approchier.
5 A male hart on le puist atachier,
L'ort, vil villain, de goute contrefait,
Qui tant de maulz et tant d'anuis nous fait!

8 Estranglé puist estre son corps des loups,
Qu'aussi ne sert il, mais que d'empeschier!
10 A quoy est bon ce vieillart plein de toux,
Fors à tencier, rechigner et crachier?
12 Dyable le puist amer ne tenir chier,
Je le hé trop, l'arné, vieil et deffait,
Qui tant de maulz et tant d'anuis nous fait!

15 Hé! qu'il dessert bien qu'on le face coux,
Le baboïn qui ne fait que cerchier
17 Par sa maison! hé quel avoir! Secoux
Un pou sa pel pour faire aler couchier,
19 Ou les degrez lui faire, sanz marchier,
Tost avaler au villain plein d'agait,
Qui tant de maulz et tant d'anuis nous fait!

⇥�⇤

ballade

Dieux! on se plaint trop durement
De ces marys, trop oy mesdire
3 D'eux, et qu'ilz sont communement
Jaloux, rechignez et pleins d'yre.
5 Mais ce ne puis je mie dire,
Car j'ay mary tout à mon vueil,
Bel et bon, et, sanz moy desdire,
Il veult trestout quanque je vueil.

9 Il ne veult fors esbatement
Et me tance quant je souspire,
11 Et bien lui plaist, s'il ne me ment,
Qu'ami aye pour moy deduire,
13 S'aultre que lui je vueil eslire;
De riens que je face il n'a dueil,
Tout lui plaist, sanz moy contredire,
Il veult trestout quanque je vueil.

17 Si doy bien vivre liement;
Car tel mary me doit souffire
19 Qui en tout mon governement
Nulle riens ne treuve à redire;
21 Et quant vers mon ami me tire
Et je lui monstre bel accueil,
Mon mary s'en rit, le doulz sire,
Il veult trestout quanque je vueil.

25 Dieu me sauve, s'il n'empire,
    Ce mary: il n'a nul pareil,
    Car chanter, dancier vueil' ou rire,
    Il veult trestout quanque je vueil.

⊁ 66 ⊀

ballade

Tres belle, je n'ose dire
La doulour et la pointure
3   Dont Amours mon cuer martire
    Pour vostre gente figure;
5   Mais du grief mal que j'endure
    Apercevoir
    Vueillez le voir.

8   Car tant doubte l'escondire
    Que la doulour que j'endure
10 Je n'ose dire n'escripre;
    Mais, sanz en faire murmure,
12 De ma grief doulour obscure
    Apercevoir
    Vueillez le voir.

15 Et vous plaise estre le mire
    De mon mal, car je vous jure
17 Que vostre, sans contredire,
    Suis et seray, c'est droiture,
19 Et se vous aim d'amour pure
    Apercevoir
    Vueillez le voir.

l'envoy

22 Si ne soiez vers moy dure,
    Ains de ma pesance sure
    Apercevoir
    Vueillez le voir.

⊀ 67 ⊁

ballade

Ayez pitié de moy, ma dame chiere;
Chiere vous ay plus que dame du monde,
3 Monde d'orgueil, ne me faites vo chiere
Chiere achater par reffus, blanche et blonde;
5 L'onde de plour m'ostez si que revoye
Voye d'avoir soulas qui me ravoye.

7 Et se je y fail, pour ce qu'à moy n'affiere,
Fiere moy mort, et en dolour parfonde
9 Fonde mon cuer et plus vivre ne quiere,
Quiere doleur ou tout meschief responde,
11 Responde à tous: Amours point ne m'envoye
Voye d'avoir soulas qui me ravoye.

13 Belle plaisant et de tous biens rentiere,
Entiere en foy, sans pareille ou seconde,
15 Com de vo serf faites, sans m'estre fiere,
Fierement non, qu'en doleur je n'affonde;
17 Fonde qui fiert mon cuer, faites que voye
Voye d'avoir soulas qui me ravoye.

l'envoy

19 Dame, vueillez que vo secours m'avoye
Voye d'avoir soulas qui me ravoye.

⋊68⋉

ballade

Qu'en puis je mais se je plains
 Et complains
Ma tres douloureuse perte,
 Trop aperte
Sur moy, car le bien qu'avoye
 Me renvoye
7 A dueil dont mon cuer est pleins.
 Si me plains,
Car à la mort suis offerte
 Sans desserte,
Par quoy regraitant, larmoye,
 L'amour moye,

13 Quant cil que doulz amis claims,
 Qui est pleins
De valour, c'est chose aperte
 Et ouverte,
Plus ne voy; c'estoit ma joye,
 Or n'esjoye
19 Riens mon cuer qui plus n'est sains
 Mais ençains
De tourment; si suis deserte
 Et aherte
A dueil sans cil que clamoye
 L'amour moye.

25 Mais trop se debat en vains
    Mon cuer vains,
  Car voye ne m'est soufferte
    Ne rouverte
  Par quoy jamais je le voye,
    Dont s'avoye
31 Mon cuer à trop durs reclaims,
    Non pas fains,
  Mais de cuer qui tout s'esserte,
    Chose est certe,
  Pour cil en qui j'affermoye
    L'amour moye:

        l'envoy

37 Estre ne puis si couverte,
    Soubz couverte,
  Que celler puisse qu'amoye
    L'amour moye.

⊁ 69 ⊁

ballade   (La Dame)
Tres doulz amy, que j'aim sur tous et prise,
Je lo Amours par qui j'ay esté prise
Et vous aussi quant vous faictes l'emprise
        Pour moy surprendre,
Car je sens ja qu'en la doulce pourprise
D'Amours, par vous, de qui je suis surprise,
Grant joye aray, et que de l'entreprise
        Bien m'en doit prendre.

9 Mais j'ay long temps fait comme mal aprise
De mettre tant dont doy estre reprise
A vous amer, Dieu lo quant m'y suis prise,
    Car sans mesprendre
Vous puis amer, car on ne me desprise
D'estre d'omme si tres vaillant esprise.
Puis qu'estes tel que nul ne vous mesprise
    Bien m'en doit prendre.

17 Or suis vostre: par droit m'avez acquise,
Plus n'est mestier que j'en soye requise,
Amours le veult, et la voye avez quise
    A mon cuer prendre
Sans mal engin par tres loyal pourquise,
Ce sçay de vray, je m'en suis bien enquise,
Et quant ainsi me plaist en toute guise
    Bien m'en doit prendre.

l'envoy

25   Ainsi aprendre
Vous m'avez fait, doulz amy, la devise
De tours d'Amours que chascun pas n'avise,
Mais puis qu'amy ay tout à ma devise
    Bien m'en doit prendre.

⊁70⊁

ballade
    (L'Amant et la Dame)
Ma dame, à Dieu vous viens dire,
Baisiez moy au departir
Et m'acolez, Dieu vous mire
Voz biens et sans repentir
M'amez, maistresse et amie,
Mon cuer laiz en vo demour.
Pour Dieu, ne m'oubliez mie,
Ma doulce loyal amour.

9 — Ha! doulz amis, onques pire
Dueil n'ot autre sans mentir,
Car mon cuer sent tel martire
Qu'il est aucques au partir.
Ce depart me rent blemie
Et de mourir en cremour.
Pour Dieu, ne m'oublïez mie,
Ma doulce loyal amour.

17 — Hé! belle dame, souffire
Doit ce dueil, plus consentir
Ne le pourroie, ostés l'ire
Qui vous fait ce mal sentir,
De pitié tout enfremie
Je revendray sans demour.
Pour Dieu, ne m'oublïez mie,
Ma doulce loyal amour.

l'envoy

25 — A Dieu te dy, suis demie
Morte, n'en verray retour.
Pour Dieu, ne m'oublïez mie,
Ma doulce loyal amour.

⤜71⤛

rondeau

Que me vault donc le complaindre
Ne moy plaindre
De la doulour que je port
4 *Quant en riens ne puet remaindre?*
Ains est graindre
Et sera jusqu'à la mort.

7 *Tant me vient doulour attaindre,*
Que restraindre
Ne puis mon grant desconfort;
10 *Que me vault donc le complaindre?*

11 Quant cil qu'amoye sanz faindre
Mort estraindre
A voulu, dont m'a fait tort;
14 Ce a fait ma joye estaindre,
Ne attaindre
Ne poz puis à nul deport;

17 *Que me vault donc le complaindre?*

⊀72⊁

rondeau

Se à faulte suis retourné
Et tourné
Vers vo corps bien atourné
4 *Et sans vëoir vo doulz oeil*
Sans orgueil,
Dame, je mourray de dueil.

7 Mon bien sera destourné,
Destourné
En langour et trestourné,
10 *Se à faulte suis retourné*

11 D'avoir autre part recueil
Dont je vueil
Mourir du mal, dont me dueil

14 *Se à faulte suis retourné.*

⊀73⊁

rondeau

Dieux
2 *Est.*

3 Quieux?
4 *Dieux.*

5 Cieulx
6 Plaist
7 *Dieux.*

virelai

En ce printemps gracïeux
D'estre gai suis envïeux
    Tout à l'onnour
De ma dame, qui vigour
    De ses doulz yeulz
Me donne, dont par lesquielx
    Vifs en baudour.

8 Toute riens fait son atour
De mener joye à son tour,
    Bois et prez tieulx
11 Sont, qu'ilz semblent de verdour
Estre vestus et de flour
    Et qui mieulx mieulx.

14 Oysiaulx chantent en maint lieux;
Pour le temps delicïeux
    Et plein d'odour
Se mettent hors de tristour
    Joennes et vieux;
Tous meinent et ris et jeux
    Ou temps paschour,

21 *En ce printemps gracïeux.*

22 Et moy n'ay je bien coulour
D'estre gay, quant la meilleur,
    Ainsi m'aist Dieux,
25 Qui soit, je sers sanz erreur,
N'à autre je n'ay favour,
    Car soubz les cieulx

28 N'a dame ou biens soient tieulx;
    Si doy estre curïeux
        Pour sa valour
    D'elle servir sanz sejour,
        Car anïeux
    Ne pourroit estre homs mortieulx
        De tel doulçour

35 *En ce printemps gracïeux.*

⊀ 75 ⊁

virelai

    Pour Dieu! ma tres doulce dame,
    Se faire se puet sans blasme
        Que vous voye,
    Je vous suppli, simple et coye
        Qui m'entame,
    Que ce soit tost, ou, par m'ame!
        Je mourroye.

8 Car venus en celle entente
    Je suis de longtain païs,
10 Et se g'y fail, belle et gente,
    Je cuideray que haïs

12 Soye de vous, car soubz lame
    Me fera mettre la flamme
        Qui maistroie
    Mon cuer. Hé las! receu soye;
        Car j'affame
    De desir qui tout m'enflamme,
        Ou que soye,

19 *Pour Dieu! ma tres doulce dame.*

20 Si ne vuelliez estre lente,
    Ou trop seray esbaïs,
22 De moy vëoir, plus ne sente
    Le mal dont suis envaïs.

24 Si puet estre que nul ame
   Nel sache, car voz diffame
       Ne vouldroie;
   Ainçois la mort soufferroie,
       Si reclame
   Vostre aide, hé las! mon cuer pasme
       Qui vous proye,

31 *Pour Dieu! ma tres doulce dame.*

Alain Chartier was born *c.* 1385 in Bayeux and died *c.* 1430 in Avignon. After his studies in the University of Paris he spent much of his life in the service of Charles VII of France. His large output of Latin and French prose works concerning the politics of his time is probably of the greatest lasting value, but he is especially celebrated for his poem in a hundred stanzas, *La Belle Dame sans Mercy,* which knew a sensational success and provoked many ripostes and continuations. Chartier also wrote some competent if uninspired lyric verse, of which five ballades and twenty-eight rondeaux survive.

⊹76⊹

ballade

  Je ne fu nez fors pour tout mal avoir
  Et soustenir les assaulz de Fortune.
3 Qu'est ce de bien? Je ne le puis savoir
  N'onques n'en eus ne n'ay joie nesune.
5 Je fusse mieulz tout mort cent fois contre une
  Que de vivre si douleureusement.
  Ce que je vueil me vient tout autrement,
  Car Fortune a pieça ma mort jurée.
  Il me desplaist de ma longue durée
  Ne je n'ay plus de vivre grant envie,
  Mais me murtrit douleur desmesurée
  Quant je ne voy ma doulce dame en vie.

13 J'ay perdu cuer, sentement et savoir.
   Plourer à part, c'est mon euvre commune.
15 Plains et regrez sont mon plus riche avoir
   Ne je ne comte en ce monde une prune.
17 Tout m'ennuye, ciel et soleil et lune,
   Et quanqui est dessoubz le firmament.
   Je desire le jour du jugement,
   Quant ma joie est soubz la tombe emmurée
   Et que la Mort m'est rude et adurée
   Qui m'a toulu celle que j'ai servie,
   Dont j'ay depuis longue peine endurée,
   Quant je ne voy ma doulce dame en vie.

25 Je n'attens riens que la mort recevoir.
   Mon cuer a pris à ma vie rancune.
27 La Mort en fait lachement son devoir
   Quant el n'occit et chascun et chascune,
29 Sans espargnier ne beauté ne peccune.
   Mais, malgré tout lour efforcéement,
   Je la requier craignant duel et torment
   Et elle soit par rigueur conjurée.
   Elas! pourquoy m'a elle procurée
   Mort à demy sans l'avoir assouvie?
   Vie en langueur, telle est ma destinée,
   Quant je ne voy ma doulce dame en vie.

⋊ 77 ⋉

ballade

   J'ay ung arbre de la plante d'amours
   Enraciné en mon cuer proprement
3 Qui ne porte fruit si non de doulours,
   Fueilles d'ennuy et flours d'encombrement.
5 Mais, puis qu'il fut planté premierement,
   Il est creü de racine et de branche,
   Que son umbre qui me porte nuisance
   Fait au dessoubz toute joie sechier,
   Et si ne puis, pour toute ma puissance,
   Autre y planter ne cellui arracier.

11 Des long tems a, l'ay arrousé de plours
Et de lermes tant doulereusement
13 Et si n'en sont les fruis de riens meillours
Ne je n'y truis gaires d'amendement.
15 Je les recueil neantmoins soigneusement.
C'est pour mon cuer amere soustenance
Qui trop mieulx fust en freche ou en souffrance
Que porter fruit qui le deüst blecier.
Mais pas ne veult l'amoureuse ordonnance
Autre y planter ne cellui arracier.

21 S'en ce printemps que les fueilles et flours
Es arbrisseaulx percent nouvellement
23 Amours vouloit moy faire ce secours
Que les branches qui font empeschement
25 Il retrenchast du tout entierement
Pour y entrer .i. rainseau de plaisance,
Il geteroit bourjons à suffisance,
Joie en ystroit, dont il n'est riens plus chier,
Et ne faudroit ja par desesperance
Autre y planter ne cellui arracier.

l'envoy

31 Ma princesce, ma premiere esperance,
Mon cuer vous sert en dure penitance.
Faittes le mal qui l'assault retrenchier
Et ne souffrez en vostre souvenance
Autre y planter ne cellui arracier.

⊁78⊁

rondeau

Triste plaisir et doulereuse joie,
Aspre doulceur, reconfort ennuyeux,
3 *Ris en plourant, souvenir oublieux,*
M'acompaignent combien que seul je soie.

5 Embuchez sont, afin qu'on ne les voie,
Dedens mon cuer en l'ombre de mes yeulx:
7 *Triste plaisir et doulereuse joie,*
Aspre doulceur, reconfort ennuyeux.

9 C'est mon tresor, ma part et ma monjoie,
De quoy Dangier est sur moy envieux.
11 Bien le sera, s'il me voit avoir mieulx,
Quant il a dueil de ce qu'Amours m'envoie.

13 *Triste plaisir et doulereuse joie,*
Aspre doulceur, reconfort ennuyeux,
15 *Ris en plourant, souvenir oublieux,*
M'acompaignent combien que seul je soie.

⊁79⊁

rondeau

Se onques deux yeulx orent telle puissance
De donner dueil et de promettre joie,
3 *J'ay de l'un plus que porter n'en pourroie*
Et de l'autre je vif en esperance.

5 Car les plus beaulz et les plus doulz de France
Ont de mon cuer fait amoureuse proie,
7 *Se onques deux yeulx orent telle puissance*
De donner dueil et de promettre joie.

9 Et se une fois l'ueil de mon cuer s'avance
Et ceulx du corps devers la belle envoie,
11 Son doulz regart qui le mien ransonnoie
Me naffre à mort et si m'offre alejance.

13 *Se onques deux yeulx orent telle puissance*
De donner dueil et de promettre joie,
15 *J'ay de l'un plus que porter n'en pourroie*
Et de l'autre je vif en esperance.

⊁{ 80 }⊁

Au feu! au feu! au feu! qui mon cuer art
Par ung brandon tiré d'un doulz regart
Tout enflambé d'ardant desir d'amours.
4 *Grace, Mercy, Confort et Bon Secours,*
Ne me laissez bruler, se Dieu vous gart.

6 Flambe, chaleur, ardeur par tout s'espart,
Estincelles et fumée s'en part.
Embrasé sui du feu qui croit tousjours.
9 *Au feu! au feu! au feu! qui mon cuer art*
Par ung brandon tiré d'un doulz regart
Tout enflambé d'ardant desir d'amours.

12 Tirez, boutez, chacez tout à l'escart
Ce dur dangier, getez de toutes part
Eaue de pitié, de larmes et de plours.
15 A l'aide, helas! je n'ay confort d'aillours;
Avancez vous ou vous vendrez trop tart!

17 *Au feu! au feu! au feu! qui mon cuer art*
Par ung brandon tiré d'un doulz regart
Tout enflambé d'ardant desir d'amours.
20 *Grace, Mercy, Confort et Bon Secours,*
Ne me laissez bruler, se Dieu vous gart.

⊁{ 81 }⊁

Belle, qui si bon cuer avez
Que jamais haÿr ne savez
Et si ne voulez riens amer,
4 *Dont vient ce que j'ay tant d'amer*
Pour vous et ne l'appercevez?

6 Malgré pitié fort me grevez
    Dont bien petit prou recevez,
    Et si ne vous en puis blamer,
9 *Belle, qui si bon cuer avez*
    Que jamais haÿr ne savez
    Et si ne voulez riens amer.

12 De mourir me parachevez
    Ou du dur mal me relevez
    Ou Amours me fait enflamer.
15 Ne me souffrez tant affamer
    Se ja bien faire me devez.

17 *Belle, qui si bon cuer avez*
    Que jamais haÿr ne savez
    Et si ne voulez riens amer,
20 *Dont vient ce que j'ay tant d'amer*
    Pour vous et ne l'appercevez?

FIFTEENTH-CENTURY LYRIC PIECES SET TO MUSIC

Although the increasing complexity of musical composition from Machaut onwards had forced a division between the poet on the one hand and the musician on the other, there were, of course, still plenty of musicians in the fifteenth century perfectly capable of writing their own verses as well as of setting to music the verses of others. There is a vast repertory of anonymous rondeaux set to music in the early part of the fifteenth century in particular.

Guillaume Dufay, Gilles Binchois, Nicolas Grenon and J. Legrant are all prominent musical figures from this time. With the exception of Binchois they all worked for some time at least in the courts of Italy and sang and composed for the papal chapel in Rome, a new trend in musical migration. As time progressed there was a constant flow of singers and composers from their excellent training in the northern cathedrals (such as Cambrai) southwards to try their fortunes in Italy. All four of the musicians selected here spent some time in the court of Burgundy, by now the most brilliant and dominating centre in French music. Grenon spent most of his life in Cambrai, where he may have taught Dufay, but spent three years in Rome from 1425. Dufay was in Italy roughly between 1420 and 1440. J. Legrant was in Rome in 1419. Only Binchois, considered the equal of Dufay and the Englishman Dunstable in his day, resisted the lure of Italy and, after a short period of service with the duke of Suffolk, remained at the court of Burgundy from about 1430 until his death in 1460.

Guillaume Dufay

⊁ 82 ⊱

rondeau

    Je ne suis plus telx que soloye;
    J'ay perdu tout solas et joye,
    Devenu suy viel et usé
4 *Et m'ont les dames refusé*
    Quant plus servir ne les povoye.

6 Jonesse me fault et monnoye
    Desquels tres enble je m'aidoye
    Et pour ce tout par supposé.
9 *Je ne suis plus telx que soloye;*
    J'ay perdu tout solas et joye,
    Devenu suy viel et usé.

12 Helas! se revenir sçavoie
    En l'estat ou primier estoye,
    Je feroye fort du rusé!
15 Et se j'en estoye acusé,
    Savés vous que responderoye?

17 *Je ne suis plus telx que soloye;*
    J'ay perdu tout solas et joye,
    Devenu suy viel et usé
20 *Et m'ont les dames refusé*
    Quant plus servir ne les povoye.

Gilles Binchois

⊁ 83 ⊱

rondeau

    Jamais tant que je vous revoye,
    Ma tres doulce dame et ma joye,
    Au cuer n'aray esbatement.
4 *Et si n'ay povoir nullement*
    De m'esjoïr com je soloye.

6   Helas! le plaisir que j'avoye
      S'en est alé, dont il m'ennoye
      Qu'il ne se peut faire autrement.

9   *Jamais tant que je vous revoye,*
      Ma tres doulce dame et ma joye,
      Au cuer n'aray esbatement.

12   Nulle riens n'est qui me resjoye
      Se non l'espoir que je vous voye
      A mon plaisir et bien briefment

15   Affin que vous sachiez coment
      Estre joyeus je ne poroye.

17   *Jamais tant que je vous revoye,*
      Ma tres doulce dame et ma joye,
      Au cuer n'aray esbatement.

20   *Et si n'ay povoir nullement*
      De m'esjoïr com je soloye.

Nicolas Grenon

⤜ 84 ⤛

rondeau

    Se je vous ay bien loyaulment amée,
    Plus c'onques mais vous ayme loiaulment.

3   *Sachiés de vray qu'à vous entierement*
   Sera de moy parfaite amour gardée.

5   De ce soiés ferme et aseürée
   Et ne dobtés qu'il en soit autrement.

7   *Se je vous ay bien loyaulment amée,*
   Plus c'onques mais vous ayme loiaulment.

9   Car la biauté dont vous estes parée,
   Le biau cler vis figuré proprement,

11 Et vos beaux yeux m'ont espris telement
   Qu'en verité autre riens ne m'agrée.

13 *Se je vous ay bien loyaulment amée,*
   Plus c'onques mais vous ayme loiaulment.
15 *Sachiés de vray qu'à vous entierement*
   Sera de moy parfaite amour gardée.

J. Legrant

⊀85⊁

rondeau

Les mesdisans ont fait raport
Aux envieux, ne sçay coment
3 *Qu'ils scevent tout certaynement*
Que ma dame sera mon confort.

5 Pour moy destruire et metre à mort
Et prendre fin aucunement
7 *Les mesdisans ont fait raport*
Aux envieux, ne sçay coment.

9 Onques de ma dame confort
Je n'eus pour vivre liement
11 Se non de la vëoir souvent;
Si m'est à trop grant desconfort.

13 *Les mesdisans ont fait raport*
Aux envieux, ne sçay coment
15 *Qu'ils scevent tout certaynement*
Que ma dame sera mon confort.

CHARLES D'ORLÉANS

Charles d'Orléans, born in 1394, was a member of the French royal family, the son of Louis, duc d'Orléans, and Valentina Visconti. In 1415 he was taken prisoner at Agincourt and was held captive in England for twenty-five years until 1440. It was during this captive exile that he composed most of his 123 ballades and 89 'chansons'. When he returned to his favourite château at Blois he led a tranquil but productive life until his death in 1465, cultivating the friendship of the poets and musicians he gathered around him, and in that period he wrote about four hundred rondeaux.

Formally, the 'chansons' are identical with the rondeaux: the distinc-tion seems to be that with a 'chanson' music was involved, something which was now an exception to the general rule. Perhaps the full refrain should be included in the 'chansons' and the shortened form in the rondeaux. In one manuscript source space is left for music, beneath the 'chanson' texts, but this was not inserted. There is no evidence that Charles d'Orléans could compose music in addition to his poetry, though it is known that he had great sympathy for musical activities.

The variety of his poetic inspiration corresponds in general to the events of his life, the theme of *Love* dominating the early poems and that of *nonchalance* the poems of his maturity.

⊁86⊁

ballade

Je ne me sçay en quel point maintenir,
Ce premier jour de May, plain de lïesse,
3 Car d'une part puis dire sans faillir
Que, Dieu mercy, j'ay loyalle maistresse,
5 Qui de tous biens a trop plus qu'a largesse.
Et si pense que, la sienne mercy,
Elle me tient son servant et amy:
Ne doy je bien donques joye mener
Et me tenir en joyeuse plaisance?
Certes ouïl, et Amour mercïer
Treshumblement, de toute ma puissance.

12 Mais d'autre part, il me couvient souffrir
Tant de douleur et de dure destresse
14 Par Fortune, qui me vient assaillir
De tous costez, qui de maulx est princesse!
16 Passer m'a fait le plus de ma jennesse,
Dieu scet comment, en doloreux party;
Et si me fait demourer en soussy,
Loings de celle par qui puis recouvrer
Le vray tresor de ma droitte esperance,
Et que je vueil obéir et amer
Treshumblement, de toute ma puissance.

23 Et pour ce, May, je vous viens requerir,
Pardonnez moy de vostre gentillesse,
25 Se je ne puis à present vous servir
Comme je doy, car je vous fais promesse;
27 J'ay bon vouloir envers vous, mais Tristesse
M'a si long temps en son dangier nourry
Que j'ay du tout Joye mis en oubly;
Si me vault mieulx seul de gens eslongier:
Qui dolent est ne sert que d'encombrance.
Pour ce, reclus me tendray en penser
Treshumblement, de toute ma puissance.

l'envoy

34 Doulx Souvenir, chierement je vous pry,
Escrivez tost ceste balade cy;
De par mon cuer la feray presenter
A ma Dame, ma seule desirance,
A qui pieça je le voulu donner
Treshumblement, de toute ma puissance.

⊁⫷87⫸⊁

ballade
    Quant je suis couschié en mon lit,
    Je ne puis en paix reposer;
3 Car toute la nuit mon cuer lit
    Ou rommant de Plaisant Penser,
5 Et me prie de l'escouter;
    Si ne l'ose desobéir
    Pour doubte de le courroucer:
    Ainsi je laisse le dormir.

9 Ce livre est tout escript
    Des fais de ma Dame sans per;
11 Souvent mon cueur de joye rit,
    Quant il les list ou oyt compter;
13 Car certes tant sont à louër
    Qu'il y prent souverain plaisir;
    Moy mesmes ne m'en puis lasser:
    Ainsi je laisse le dormir.

17 Se mes yeulx demandent respit
    Par Sommeil qui les vient grever,
19 Il les tense par grant despit,
    Et si ne les peut surmonter:
21 Il ne cesse de soupirer
    A part soy; j'ay lors, sans mentir,
    Grant paine de le rapaiser:
    Ainsi je laisse le dormir.

l'envoy

25 Amour, je ne puis gouverner
Mon cueur; car tant vous veult servir
Qu'il ne scet jour ne nuit cesser:
Ainsi je laisse le dormir.

⊁ 88 ⊁

ballade

Ardant desir de vëoir ma maistresse
A assailly de nouvel le logis
3 De mon las cueur, qui languist en tristesse,
Et puis dedens par tout a le feu mis.
5 En grant doubte certainement je suis
Qu'il ne soit pas legierement estaint,
Sans grant grace: si vous pry, Dieu d'Amours,
Sauvez mon cueur, ainsi qu'avez fait maint:
Je l'oy crïer piteusement secours.

10 J'ay essayé par lermes à largesse
De l'estaindre, mais il n'en vault que pis;
12 C'est feu gregeois, ce croy je, qui ne cesse
D'ardre, s'il n'est estaint par bon avis.
14 Au feu, au feu, courez, tous mes amis!
S'aucun de vous, comme lasche, remaint
Sans y aler, je le hé pour tousjours;
Avanciez vous, nul de vous ne soit faint,
Je l'oy crïer piteusement secours.

19 S'il est ainsi mort par vostre peresse,
Je vous requier, au moins, tant que je puis,
21 Chascun de vous donnez lui une messe,
Et j'ay espoir que brief ou paradis
23 Des amoureux sera moult hault assis,
Comme martir et treshonnoré saint,
Qui a tenu de Loyauté le cours:
Grant tourment a, puis que si fort se plaint;
Je l'oy crïer piteusement secours.

⊁ 89 ⊁

ballade

Dangier, je vous giette mon gant,
Vous apellant de traïson,
3   Devant le Dieu d'Amours puissant
Qui me fera de vous raison:
5   Car vous m'avez mainte saison
Fait douleur à tort endurer,
Et me faittes loings demourer
De la nompareille de France.
Mais vous l'avez tousjours d'usance
De grever loyaulx amoureux,
Et pour ce que je sui l'un d'eulx,
Pour eulx et moy prens la querelle;
Par Dieu, vilain, vous y mourrés
Par mes mains, point ne le vous celle,
S'à Léauté ne vous rendés!

16   Comment avez vous d'orgueil tant
Que vous osez, sans achoison,
18   Tourmenter aucun vray amant
Qui, de cueur et d'entencïon,
20   Sert Amours sans condicïon?
Certes moult estes à blasmer,
Pensez doncques de l'amender,
En laissant vostre mal vueillance,
Et, par treshumble repentance,
Alez crïer mercy à ceulx
Que vous avez fais douloureux,
Et qui vous ont trouvé rebelle.
Autrement pour seur vous tenez
Que de gage je vous appelle,
S'à Léauté ne vous rendés!

31 Vous estes tous temps mal pensant
Et plain de faulse soupeçon;
33 Ce vous vient de mauvais talant,
Nourry en courage felon.

35 Que mal ou ennuy vous fait on,
Se par amours on veult amer,
Pour plus aise le temps passer
En lyée, joyeuse Plaisance?
C'est gracïeuse desirance.
Pour ce, faulx, vilain, orgueillieux,
Changiez voz vouloirs outragieux,
Ou je vous feray guerre telle
Que, sans faillir, vous trouverés
Qu'elle vauldra pis que mortelle,
S'à Léauté ne vous rendés!

⊁{ 90 }⊱

ballade

J'oy estrangement
Plusieurs gens parler,
3 Qui trop mallement
Se plaingnent d'amer;
5 Car legierement,
Sans paine porter,
Vouldroyent briefment
A fin amener
Tout leur pensement.

10 C'est fait follement
D'ainsy desirer;
12 Car qui loyaument
Veulent acquester
14 Bon guerdonnement,
Maint mal endurer
Leur fault, et souvent
A rebours trouver
Tout leur pensement.

III

19 S'Amour humblement
  Veulent honnourer,
21 Et soingneusement
  Servir, sans fausser,
23 Des biens largement
  Leur fera donner;
  Mais, premierement,
  Il veult esprouver
  Tout leur pensement.

⊀91⊁

ballade

L'emplastre de Nonchaloir,
Que sus mon cueur pieça mis,
3 M'a guery, pour dire voir,
  Si nettement que je suis
5 En bon point; ne je ne puis
  Plus avoir, jour de ma vie,
  L'amoureuse maladie.

8 Si font mes yeulx leur povoir
  D'espïer par le pays,
10 S'ilz pourroient plus vëoir
  Plaisant Beauté, qui jadis
12 Fut l'un de mes ennemis,
  Et mist en ma compaignie
  L'amoureuse maladie.

15 Mes yeulx tense, main et soir,
  Mais ilz sont si treshastis,
17 Et trop plains de leur vouloir:
  Au fort, je les metz au pis,
19 Facent selon leur advis;
  Plus ne crains, dont Dieu mercie,
  L'amoureuse maladie.

l'envoy

22 Quant je voy en doleur pris
    Les amoureux, je m'en ris;
    Car je tiens pour grant folie
    L'amoureuse maladie.

⪪ 92 ⪫

Je meurs de soif en couste la fontaine;
Tremblant de froit ou feu des amoureux;
3 Aveugle suis, et si les autres maine;
    Povre de sens, entre saichans l'un d'eulx;
5 Trop negligent, en vain souvent songneux;
    C'est de mon fait une chose faiée,
    En bien et mal par Fortune menée.

8 Je gaingne temps, et pers mainte sepmaine;
    Je joue et ris, quant me sens douloureux;
10 Desplaisance j'ay d'esperance plaine;
    J'atens bon eur en regret engoisseux;
12 Rien ne me plaist, et si suis desireux;
    Je m'esjoïs, et cource à ma pensée,
    En bien et mal par Fortune menée.

15 Je parle trop, et me tais à grant paine;
    Je m'esbaÿs, et si suis couraigeux;
17 Tristesse tient mon confort en demaine;
    Faillir ne puis, au mains à l'un des deulx;
19 Bonne chiere je faiz quant je me deulx;
    Maladie m'est en santé donnée,
    En bien et mal par Fortune menée.

l'envoy

22 Prince, je dy que mon fait maleureux
    Et mon prouffit aussi avantageux,
    Sur ung hasart j'asserray quelque année,
    En bien et mal par Fortune menée.

⊁ 93 ⊁

rondeau
(chanson)

Belle, se c'est vostre plaisir
De me vouloir tant enrichir
De reconfort et de lïesse,
4 *Je vous requier, comme maistresse,*
Ne me laissiez du tout mourir.

6 Car je n'ay vouloir ne desir,
Fors de vous loyaument servir
Sans espargnier dueil ne tristesse,
9 *Belle, se c'est vostre plaisir*
De me vouloir tant enrichir
De reconfort et de lïesse.

12 Et s'il vous plaist à l'acomplir,
Vueilliez tant seulement bannir
D'avec vostre doulce jeunesse,
15 Dolent refus qui trop me blesse,
Dont bien vous me povez guerir.

17 *Belle, se c'est vostre plaisir*
De me vouloir tant enrichir
De reconfort et de lïesse,
20 *Je vous requier, comme maistresse,*
Ne me laissiez du tout mourir.

⊁ 94 ⊁

rondeau
(chanson)

Je ne prise point telz baisiers
Qui sont donnez par contenance,
3 *Ou par maniere d'acointance;*
Trop de gens en sont parçonniers.

5 On en peut avoir par milliers,
A bon marchié, grant habondance.
7 *Je ne prise point telz baisiers*
Qui sont donnez par contenance.

9 Mais savez vous lesquelz sont chiers?
Les privez, venans par plaisance;
11 Tous autres ne sont, sans doubtance,
Que pour festier estrangiers.

13 *Je ne prise point telz baisiers*
Qui sont donnez par contenance,
15 *Ou par maniere d'acointance;*
Trop de gens en sont parçonniers.

⊁ 95 ⊁

rondeau
(chanson)

Le voulez vous
Que vostre soye?
3 *Rendu m'octroye,*
Pris ou recours.

5 Ung mot pour tous,
Bas qu'on ne l'oye:
7 *Le voulez vous*
Que vostre soye?

9 Maugré jalous,
Foy vous tendroye;
11 Or sa, ma joye,
Accordons nous.

13 *Le voulez vous*
Que vostre soye?
15 *Rendu m'octroye,*
Pris ou recours.

⊁{96}⊱

rondeau
(chanson)

Crevez moy les yeulx
Que ne voye goutte,
3 Car trop je redoubte
Beaulté en tous lieulx.

5 Ravir jusqu'aus cieulx
Veult ma joye toute;
7 Crevez moy les yeulx
Que ne voye goutte.

9 D'elle me gard Dieulx,
Affin qu'en sa route
11 Jamais ne me boute;
N'esse pour le mieulx?

13 Crevez moy les yeulx
Que ne voye goutte,
15 Car trop je redoubte
Beaulté en tous lieulx.

⊁{97}⊱

rondeau

Le temps a laissié son manteau
De vent, de froidure et de pluye,
3 Et s'est vestu de brouderie,
De soleil luyant, cler et beau.

5 Il n'y a beste, ne oyseau,
Qu'en son jargon ne chante ou crie:
7 Le temps a laissié son manteau!

8 Riviere, fontaine et ruisseau
Portent, en livrée jolie,
10 Gouttes d'argent d'orfaverie;
Chascun s'abille de nouveau:

12 Le temps a laissié son manteau.

⊁ 98 ⊁

rondeau

Le monde est ennuyé de moy,
Et moy pareillement de lui;
3 *Je ne congnois rien au jour d'ui*
Dont il me chaille que bien poy.

5 Dont quanque devant mes yeulx voy,
Puis nommer anuy sur anuy;
7 *Le monde est ennuyé de moy.*

8 Cherement se vent bonne foy,
A bon marché n'en a nulluy;
10 Et pour ce, se je suis cellui
Qui m'en plains, j'ay raison pour quoy:

12 *Le monde est ennuyé de moy.*

⊁ 99 ⊁

rondeau

Temps et temps m'ont emblé Jennesse,
Et laissé és mains de Viellesse
Ou vois mon pouvre pain querant;
4 *Aage ne me veult, tant ne quant,*
Donner l'aumosne de Lïesse.

6 Puis qu'elle se tient ma maistresse,
Demander ne luy puis promesse,
Pour ce, n'enquerons plus avant.
9 *Temps et temps m'ont emblé Jennesse.*

10 Je n'ay repast que de Foiblesse,
Couchant sur paille de Destresse,
Suy je bien payé maintenant
13 De mes jennes jours cy devant?
Nennil, nul n'est qui le redresse:

15 *Temps et temps m'ont emblé Jennesse.*

⊁ 100 ⊱

virelai

Yver, vous n'estes qu'un villain,
Esté est plaisant et gentil,
En tesmoing de May et d'Avril
Qui l'acompaignent soir et main.

5 Esté revest champs, bois et fleurs,
Et de sa livrée de verdure
7 Et de maintes autres couleurs,
Par l'ordonnance de Nature.

9 Mais vous, Yver, trop estes plain
De nege, vent, pluye et grezil;
On vous deust banir en essil.
Sans point flater, je parle plain:

13 *Yver, vous n'estes qu'un vilain!*

NOTES

1   This early ballade has only one line set to the first section of the music, as opposed to the more usual two lines to be found in other ballades by Lescurel and most later examples. Another feature characteristic of the earliest stage is the shortened penultimate line of three syllables. Later, the shortened line, if any, invariably occurred at the *beginning* of the second music section. Moreover, the early taste for such a scheme as eight and three syllables to the line was to be superseded by the middle of the fourteenth century by a preference for ten and seven syllables. The form here is:

Music: I I II

Text: $a_8a_8a_8b_8b_3B_8$

The text is in many ways typical of the tradition of the courtly lyric; either the allegorical figure of *Amours* is to console the lover's anguish or *Mort* is to put an end to it. Here, though, the words are put into the lady's mouth as she sighs for her absent 'dous amis' and this at least is closer to what is sometimes called 'Ovidian' love than to *amour courtois,* for the lady has descended from her pedestal and position of superiority and suffers equally with the man from the pangs and the malady of love. True to tradition, the course of true love has been disturbed by the 'lozengier', jealous persons and trouble-makers, here called the 'mauparliere gent'.

See music example no. 1.

2   This ballade displays a further characteristic of the earliest stage, that of having a refrain *two* lines long. Later in the fourteenth century it is rare to find a refrain occupying more than the final line of the stanza. The seven-syllable line throughout is also seldom to be found later on.

The text treats another basic ingredient of the *amour courtois* situation, that of 'unattainability' either for social or for geographical reasons, of 'amour de loin', which was celebrated above all by the twelfth-century troubadour Jaufré Rudel. Because of his 'éloignance' from the 'très dous pays' where his lady dwells, the poet is in torment: his face is pale but he has to keep his love in secret. However, he consoles himself with memories of his lady's beauty and with the *hope* that he may yet receive her love.

3   This rondeau is of the most straightforward type, eight lines long. Again, it uses the early seven-syllable line. The form has a long history, having emerged from early dance lyrics (as did the ballade and virelai a little later); examples of six-line rondeaux, without the preliminary refrain, are known from the twelfth century and both six-line and eight-line types occur side by side among the lyric interpolations in Jean Renart's romance of *Guillaume de Dôle,* written in the early years of the thirteenth century. Adam de la Hale, at the end of the thirteenth century, exploited the form skilfully, giving numerous formal elaborations and also the earliest polyphonic rondeau musical

settings. It has to be realised that throughout the whole of the early troubadour and trouvère period until Adam de la Hale, musical settings were normally monodic, a single (though not always a simple) melody for a solo voice. Adam de la Hale wrote both monodic *chansons* and polyphonic rondeaux and motets for three voices in the new style and thus is a vitally important figure in the development of the musical side of the trouvère art. Lescurel left one polyphonic rondeau setting in a style similar to that of Adam de la Hale, but the rest of his verse has survived only with unaccompanied melodies.

The text this time presents the lover's direct appeal to his lady.

4 The eleven-line rondeau was a form exploited by Adam de la Hale, Jehan de Lescurel and Jehan Acart at the turn of the thirteenth and fourteenth centuries but is very rarely to be seen thereafter, though Machaut and Froissart give examples (poems 22 and 41). This mixed metre, too, of five and seven syllables, starting with the shorter line, was something seldom to be encountered in the musical settings of Machaut and his followers (though Machaut provides several interesting variants in ballade form) and this type of technique was only to reappear in the works of Christine de Pisan, at the turn of the fourteenth and fifteenth centuries, when the steadying influence of musical considerations had been removed.

The form is:

Music: I II   I I   I II   I II

Text: $A_5B_5B_7$ a_5A_5 $a_5b_5b_7$ $A_5B_5B_7$

The poet here again makes a direct appeal to his lady.

See music example no. 2.

5 This virelai is possibly Lescurel's finest composition. Again the poet appeals to his lady and protests his devotion to her, but the four-line refrain employs an especially pleasing image: the poet sends his lady ten times more amorous greetings than it would take flowers piled up to reach the sky. More exciting still is the discovery of an acrostic (reappearances of the refrain are to be ignored): DAME, JEHAN DE LESCUREL VOUS SALUE. It was a popular practice of the time to introduce the name of the poet or of a patron into the first letters of each line, but it is something of a rarity to find a complete amorous message such as this.

The form is interesting in that eight-syllable lines are used for the first music section but seven-syllable lines for the second music section:

Music: I   II II   I   I

Text: $A_8B_8A_8B_8$ $c_7d_7c_7d_7$ $a_8b_8a_8b_8$ $A_8B_8A_8B_8$ etc.

See music example no. 3.

JEHAN ACART DE HESDIN

6 The ballades of Jehan Acart, contained in *La Prise amoureuse* of 1332, continue to show the flexible approach possible within the general framework. This example is unusual in that the refrain line, of seven syllables, is shorter than all the preceding lines in the stanza, which have eight syllables each.

This is a further prayer for mercy from the lover to his lady.

7 Mixed metres are again used in this ballade, in a pleasing pattern of long-short-long plus a final refrain line. The form here is relatively unusual in that three (and not two) lines appear set to the first music section; Machaut gives extended examples on a similar pattern (e.g. poem 15). Form:

Music: I I II
Text: $a_7a_3b_7a_7a_3b_7c_7c_3d_7D_7$

8 An eleven-line rondeau with seven syllables to the line in which the poet proclaims how much he is in the power of *Amours*.

9 A further possibility is the thirteen-line rondeau, though this is rarely encountered:

Music: I II I I I II I II
Text $A_7B_7B_7$ $a_7b_7A_7B_7$ $a_7b_7b_7$ $A_7B_7B_7$

Machaut gives some examples of this type (e.g. poem 23).

10 This is a sixteen-line type rondeau, but very different from the standard sixteen-line type of the fifteenth century. In this example there are lines of four different lengths:

Music: I II I I I II I II
Text: $A_7B_5A_8B_2$ $a_7b_5A_7B_5$ $a_7b_5a_8b_2$ $A_7B_5A_8B_2$

A poem in praise of his lady's beauty.

GUILLAUME DE MACHAUT

11 This is the typical pattern of the mid- and late fourteenth-century ballade of Machaut and his followers. Ten syllables is now the fashion: if there is to be a shorter line, the number of syllables in it must be seven and it must occur at the beginning of the second music section. Two lines are regularly set to the first music section. The refrain is one line long:

Music: I I II
Text: $a_{10}b_{10}a_{10}b_{10}c_7c_{10}d_{10}D_{10}$

The length of the text set to the second music section may vary; here it is four lines, but as time progressed longer passages were tried (e.g. poem 30, by J. de Noyon) and, when music had vanished from the scene, ballades with stanzas up to thirteen lines long are to be encountered (e.g. poem 43 from *Le Livre des Cent Ballades*) or even fifteen lines long (e.g. poem 89 by Charles d'Orléans).

The rose image here may well have been inspired incidentally by the famous *Roman de la Rose*, but Machaut takes the symbol and shows with great delicacy his fears that fickle Fortune may destroy the fragrant flower, all he has left in his 'vergier'. See music example no. 4.

12 Here Machaut uses the octosyllabic line, which by now seems almost an anachronism —perhaps there was something consciously old-fashioned in his choice of this metre.

Taking Ovid as his source, Machaut uses classical mythology to good advantage: never was the terrible serpent slain by Phebus as cruel as his lady when she will not grant him mercy. The seven heads of the serpent are all allegorical impediments to the lover's progress: Refusal, Disdain, Spite, Shame, Fear, Harshness, Danger; worst of all, his lady laughs at him and enjoys his torment when he seeks her love.

Machaut and his followers made great use of classical heroes and mythological events, to such an extent, in fact, that the procedure becomes stereotyped and tends to lose its effect.

It is interesting to compare this poem to the version of it by a follower of Machaut, Magister Franciscus (poem 27).

13 Using his standard ballade form, Machaut here displays a sense of humour: the poem is a tirade against the month of March when, Machaut tells us, he contracted the gout. April, however, with its warmth and blossom, is praised for effecting the cure.

This poem, from the *Louange des Dames*, was not set to music.

14 A further ballade without music from the *Louange des Dames*, this gives us the colour symbolism of the middle ages, taken very seriously at the time: yellow is falsehood, white is joy, green is fickleness, red is ardour, black is mourning, but azure (or blue) is superior to them all since it signifies loyalty. It is the lady who is speaking and she says that she will dress herself in blue as a sign to her lover that she is constant.

15 A further ballade, without music in the *Louange des Dames* but set to music among the *Ballades notées*. Here Machaut does exploit the older mixed metres and shorter lines, in this case of seven and three syllables. This poem may be compared to the Jehan Acart example, poem 7, but Machaut expands the form further by repeating the *second,* as well as the first music section (cf. notes to poem 16 below).

16 This *Ballade notée* is interesting formally because it, too, exploits the older mixed metres and shorter lines, here of seven, four and three syllables. What is more, *both* music sections are repeated, a feature which is only very occasionally encountered in the compositions of the post-Machaut generation:

Music: I   I   II   II
Text: $a_7a_4a_3b_7a_7a_4a_3b_7b_4b_3a_7b_4b_3A_7$

Machaut is clearly taking a delight in formal elaboration and the result is an exceptionally long stanza of fourteen lines.

See music example no. 5.

17 & 18   These two items belong together as 'double ballade': it is vital to appreciate that in the musical setting the two texts (three stanzas each) are performed *simul-taneously* by two singers, with a further two independent instruments as accompani-ment. The polytextual technique of setting different sets of words to be sung at one and the same time was the basic characteristic of the great semi-ecclesiastical motet form of the thirteenth and fourteenth centuries and we know from a few examples by Machaut and his followers that attempts were sometimes made to apply this technique to the lyric *formes fixes*.

Machaut tells his lady Péronne, in the *Livre du Voir Dit,* a collection of letters and poems which passed between the couple, that the ballade 'Ne quier vëoir' was sent to him by Thomas Paien (a lecturer at the Sorbonne) and that he had written a companion to it, 'Quant Theseüs', and set the two texts together to music for her delight. The technique of 'Quant Theseüs' does seem to be superior to the fairly banal mythological listing in 'Ne quier vëoir' and both are certainly superior to Froissart's adaptation (poem 36).

A performance of this piece, together with other lyric compositions by Machaut and his *Messe de Nostre Dame,* may be heard on the Archiv record no. 14063. In this case, of course, the two texts are deliberately constructed on the same pattern and share the same refrain: this need not necessarily be so, however, and in the motet itself the simultaneously performed texts are very often most disparate both in content and in form and sometimes even in language. After the confusion of the two texts in the main part of the stanzas, Machaut produces a splendid effect of clarity as the two voices come together for the refrain, giving extra point to his catalogue of legen-dary personages and events: 'Je voy assez, puis que je voy ma dame'.

Compare the similar double ballade construction by Eustache Deschamps, his lament on the death of Machaut, poems 50 and 51.

See music example no. 6.

19   Machaut calls this example, which has no music, from the *Louange des Dames,* a 'ballade double'. It is in effect exactly twice the length of a normal ballade, six stanzas instead of three. The lover and the lady exchange their mutual laments on the forces which keep them apart in alternate stanzas, three stanzas in all for the lover, who begins, and three for the lady. Machaut here uses the older seven-syllable line.

There are several later examples of this type, for example by Christine de Pisan and by François Villon.

20   From the *Louange des Dames,* this is a typical *chanson royal,* a form related to the ballade but, indeed, closer still to the traditional troubadour *canso* and trouvère *chanson* in its number of stanzas (usually five), their general length (nine lines here), its absence of

refrain and its final *envoi*. The *envoi*, with its appeal to the *Prince*, is indicative of the circumstances of performance, in a Puy or gathering of poets and their judges. From Deschamps onwards, when poetry had become disassociated from music, the ballade form often adopted this traditional *envoi*. It is clear that there could be no question of a ballade with *envoi* being set to music, since there is no place for the *envoi* in the musical structure.

The text shows the poet in a conventional situation: he dares not declare his passion to his lady, dares not send anyone else with the message (because of the need for secrecy), and yet longs for her to show him mercy.

21   This eight-line rondeau with ten syllables to the line, set to music, is also found in the *Louange des Dames* and in *Le Voir Dit*; it is an enigma: the numbers relate to the letters of the alphabet (i and j are counted as one letter)—17:R / 5:E / 13:N / 14:O / 15:P—this gives RENOP, which must then be shuffled and some letters repeated to give PERONNE, the name of the young lady Péronne d'Armentières to whom Machaut paid so much attention in his old age. This type of ingenuity is frequently to be encountered in mediaeval art, and numerical complexity has, of course, particular relevance to the musical side of lyric composition.

See music example no. 7.

22   An example of the older, eleven-line rondeau with seven syllables from the *Louange des Dames*. The text advocates the need for loyalty in amorous affairs. There is no music set to this poem.

23   An example of the rare thirteen-line rondeau with seven syllables (cf. poem 9 by Jehan Acart). The poem is set to music and also appears in the *Louange des Dames*; it compares the lady to the fragrance and flowers of Spring.

24   This virelai conforms to the standard pattern in its musical structure (cf. poem 5 by Jehan de Lescurel) but illustrates the tendency of the mid- and late fourteenth-century virelai to length and elaboration in the text. No less than seven lines are set to the first music section as the refrain and these already set up a pattern of varying metre in seven and four syllables. Three lines occupy the second music section and the whole form is repeated three times in all, giving a very extended piece sixty-seven lines long. A complete performance might take up a good ten minutes:

Music: I   II   II   I   I
Text: $A_7A_7B_4B_7A_4A_7B_4$ $b_7b_7a_4b_7b_7a_4$ $a_7a_7b_4b_7a_4a_7b_4$ $A_7A_7B_4B_7A_4A_7B_4$ etc.

It is, however, important to note that of his thirty-three virelais set to music, Machaut set twenty-five monodically, i.e. in the older tradition (cf. Lescurel's monodic settings).

The lover here makes a striking comparison: the hardness of his lady towards him is greater than that of a diamond or a lodestone.

See music example no. 8.

25 Machaut here gives an even more elaborate version of the virelai, with mixed metres of two, three and seven syllables and extended to a total length of seventy-four lines. The lover again protests his loyalty and devotion—he does not deserve the disdain in which his lady holds him.

THE POST-MACHAUT GENERATION

26 Ballades by the poet-musicians following Machaut rarely deviate from the standard pattern with ten syllables to the line; occasionally the fifth line is shorter, with seven syllables. This ballade, by P. des Molins, was one of the most celebrated pieces of its time and was incorporated into a tapestry made in Arras about 1420 (reproduced in H. Besseler, *Die Musik des Mittelalters und der Renaissance*, Potsdam, 1931, facing p. 136, and E. Droz & G. Thibault, *Poètes et musiciens du 15e siècle*, Paris, 1924, facing p. 21): the scene is a flower-spangled clearing. Through abundant foliage the walls of a great castle are visible. In the centre sits a nobleman, richly clothed and holding out a long roll of music for a young woman at the right who is performing on the harp. The music goes along the length of the *rotulus,* quite unlike any of the known manuscript sources, but this is purely for the purposes of the tapestry, for the words 'De ce que fol pensé' can be seen, worked in bold letters. It is quite likely that the nobleman is singing to the lady's accompaniment.

The text is a further example of 'love from afar', for the poet has been obliged to 'languir en estrange contrée'; could this be more than a literary convention though, for P. des Molins certainly did leave his native northern France? It shows affinities with works by both Machaut and Deschamps and has been attributed on occasion to each of them; however, there seems to be no good reason for denying P. des Molins' right to the poem.

See music example no. 9.

27 Composed in honour of Gaston Phébus, this ballade by Magister Franciscus is closely related to Machaut's ballade 'Phyton, le mervilleus serpent' (poem 12):

a Franciscus: 1. Phiton, Phiton, beste très veneneuse
    Machaut: 1. Phiton, le mervilleus serpent
b Franciscus: 5. De par Phébus le très bel
    Machaut: 2. Que Phébus de sa flesche occit
c Franciscus: 9. Bien te descrit Ovide, si crueuse
    Machaut: 4. Si com Ovides le descrit

It should be noted that *Phébus* has changed significance in the Franciscus piece and is more than the purely learned reference in Machaut's poem. The comte de Foix used the name 'Fébus' from 1360 onwards and so the composition must have been written after that date. The rhyme scheme and the syllabic structures of the two poems do not correspond.

28 By J. Cuvelier, a ballade in honour of Gaston Phébus.

29   By Philipoctus de Caserta, this ballade was written about 1382 to celebrate the departure from Avignon of the duc d'Anjou with his army to regain the kingdom of Naples, which had been taken from Jeanne I by the treacherous Charles Durazzo. The enigmatic refrain 'O couvert de LIS' reveals the name LOIS (duc d'Anjou). See music example no. 10.

30   According to the source manuscript (Chantilly, Musée Condé, 1047), this text was written by J. de Noyon but set to music by J. Simon de Haspre. The ballade is notable for its length (stanzas eleven lines long) and the wit and originality of its theme: bad temper can inspire one to good works and it is good to let off steam as long as no one is hurt by it! Deschamps, too, gives a text on the 'société des fumeux'. There is great vivacity in J. de Noyon's play on words—'Je sui fumeux plains de fumée', 'Home fumeux peut en fumant mover', etc.

31   This is Senleches' ballade composed on the death of Eleanor d'Aragon in 1382. The poet clearly feels that further patronage in the court of Castile is unlikely and there is a note of pathos in his appeal to his fellow minstrels (some have said to his wife) to set out again on their uncertain way of life—'Fuions querir no vie non seüre'. See music example no. 11.

32   This charming rondeau is in the basic eight-line form which predominated in the late fourteenth century. Like the majority of works of the time it is anonymous; indeed there is a great danger in an anthology of this kind of distorting the picture— with the exception of the greatest writers, such as Guillaume de Machaut and Christine de Pisan with their specially illuminated collections, it is almost something out of the ordinary to know the poet's name. Anonymity, however, does not by any means imply inferiority. See music example no. 12.

33   A further anonymous eight-line rondeau, this time a religious text with the Virgin Mary as its subject.

34   This virelai by Grimace is typical of the late fourteenth-century form in its elaborate mixing of metres (eight, seven, six, five and four syllables), the number of lines set to each section, and its effect of bustle and excitement here not far removed from the 'realistic virelai' type. The metaphors here are military: 'Alarme', 'Wacarme' are battle cries; the lady is to take up arms to drive away the poet's 'dolour obscure'. See music example no. 13.

35   A virelai by Trebor, again showing all the typical characteristics of the late fourteenth-century type. This is an example of the 'realistic virelai', introducing stylized imitations of bird song (a feature very reminiscent of the older French reverdies). This form has much in common with the Italian caccia and a relatively rare French

form, the *chace*. Birds warbling in thickets, street scenes, people rushing to put out a fire: lively subjects such as these are the inspiration of the realistic virelai. The music, with its bird song and hunting calls, often presents excellent early examples of painting in sound.

The poet here turns the form skilfully to fit his intentions: the nightingale and the skylark are to sing his song and present his message of love to his lady for him.

JEHAN FROISSART

36 Froissart here bases a ballade on a composition by Machaut (poems 17 and 18). There is no music, of course, and so there is no question of a 'double ballade' setting. The 'Ne quier vëoir' ballade is given in shorter form by Froissart (seven decasyllabic lines) and the original refrain is retained. The poet's aim seems to be to retell the ballade but as far as possible to use *different* examples from mythology than those chosen by Machaut; this leads to a relatively sterile 'catalogue' poem.

37 A longer decasyllabic ballade by Froissart, comparable perhaps to Machaut's 'De toutes flours' (poem 11). This ballade occurs in *Le Paradys d'Amours,* but is also numbered among Froissart's separately composed ballades, where there is a different third stanza:

19 Mé trop grant doel me croist et renouvelle,
   Quant me souvient de la douce flourette,
21 Car enclose est dedens une tourelle,
   S'a une haie au devant de li faitte,
23 Qui nuit et jour m'empece et contrarie.
   Més s'Amours voelt estre de mon aïe,
   Jà pour creniel, pour tour, ne par garite,
   Je ne lairai qu'à occoison ne die:
   Sus toutes flours j'aime la margherite.

The name Margherite presumably held some special significance for Froissart and the flower ballade he builds up on it is composed with skill. The reference may be to Marguérite de Bourgogne, married in a celebrated double wedding at Cambrai in 1385, but we should remember that Froissart gives the name of his first love as Marguerite in *L'Espinette Amoureuse* (ed. A. Fourrier, l. 3389) and also composed a *Dittie de la flour de la Margherite,* reminiscent of Machaut's *Dit de la Marguerite.*

38 This ten-line, ten-syllable ballade is the first in the *Trésor amoureux* (1396), an allegorical tale in the form of a debate between an 'écuyer' and the poet. Froissart explains to his readers that he has drawn up an index ('table') of the ballades and their refrains contained in his book, each one with a reference number, so that one can swiftly turn to a ballade on whatever subject one fancies within the broad division *'D'armes, d'amours et de moralité'.*

This refrain is interesting, since it seems to be deliberately related to an earlier and well-known one, '*Armes, Amours, Dames, Chevalerie*': these words may have been a motto of the king of Aragon and a ballade with this refrain was addressed to that monarch in 1388 by Trebor ('En seumeillant m'avint une vesion'); it reoccurs in the first line of Deschamps' lament on the death of Machaut in 1377 (poem 50; see notes).

39 Also from the *Trésor amoureux,* this piece takes up the theme of 'Armes et Amours' from the refrain of the preceding item: a question is put—'How should one best comport oneself in love and in combat?'—and the answer given—'in loyalty and in humility'.

The form is extremely interesting. Froissart achieves something original and unique by subtly combining the structures of the rondeau and the ballade, though the idea must have its roots in the popular thirteenth- and early fourteenth-century form of the *Motet enté* or 'grafted Motet' in which, for example, the two lines of a rondeau refrain might be taken as the first and last lines of a Motet text and considerable new material interpolated between them.

Using the eight-syllable line throughout, Froissart first gives a standard eight-line rondeau. This is then expanded into three ballade stanzas. The final line of the rondeau acts as the ballade refrain throughout; line 1 of the rondeau opens the first ballade stanza; line 2 of the rondeau, since it is also the final line, is already accounted for; line 3 of the rondeau opens the second ballade stanza; line 4 of the rondeau, since it is also the first line, is already accounted for; line 5 of the rondeau opens the third and final ballade stanza; only one line of the rondeau remains unused in the ballade, line 6, and this is now inserted as the ante-penultimate in the final ballade stanza.

40 A further example of the combined rondeau-ballade from the *Trésor amoureux.* This is similar to the preceding item, but ten-syllable lines are used and this time the ballade stanzas, of ten lines each, are two lines longer than the original rondeau.

The poem is in praise of Love.

41 An eleven-line rondeau in seven-syllable lines, a type foreign to Froissart's musical contemporaries but known in earlier years (cf. poems 4 and 8). It is taken from *Le Paradys d'Amours,* an allegorical composition relating a dream in which the poet is assailed by Despair but, thanks to the protection of *Plaisance* and *Esperance,* is introduced into the *clos* of the King of Love and, from then on, into an orchard where his lady places a *chapelet* upon his head, with words of amorous encouragement The poet here says that one must accept whatever one is given by *Amours.*

42 A virelai from *L'Espinette amoureuse,* Froissart's description of his childhood and first experience of love. The theme here is once more of unrequited love in absence.

LE LIVRE DES CENT BALLADES

43 Ballade XLIX from the *Livre des Cent Ballades*; the experienced knight sums up his advice on the need for loyalty in love.

    The form is notable for its length (the stanzas have thirteen lines each). This increased length in what was, historically, the second music section, is, in the ballade, one of the most notable consequences of the removal of the musical context.

44 The final ballade $\overline{C}$ from the *Livre des Cent Ballades,* in which further debate on *loyauté* versus *fausseté* is invited from the court.

    The form shows a pleasing pattern of eight- and four-syllable lines, reminiscent of some of Machaut's compositions (cf. poem 15).

45 The contribution among the *Responces des Ballades* of the duc de Berry, uncle of Charles VI and Louis d'Orléans. He sits neatly on the fence in the debate between *loyauté* and *fausseté* with his declaration that '*On peut l'un dire et l'autre doit on faire*', a duplicity which is said to be well in keeping with his character.

    This ballade is in the standard form as we have seen it so far, but it is interesting to note that, whereas all the earlier *Cent Ballades* have three stanzas and a regular refrain line, the slightly later *Responces,* written, of course, when the original poets had returned to France from their campaigns in the Middle East, display a distinct advancement in structural ideas: one by Louis d'Orléans (a good example to his future poet son, Charles d'Orléans) has five stanzas; another has five stanzas and *envoi*, as in the *chanson royal*; three others have three stanzas and *envoi*, the type to be much exploited by non-musician poets in the late fourteenth and fifteenth centuries (cf. notes to poem 20).

EUSTACHE DESCHAMPS

46 This ballade, 'contre ceux qui lui empruntent ses livres', illustrates a concept of formal perfection to be encountered in several fifteenth-century treatises of versification, namely that a ballade in decasyllables should have stanzas ten lines long. The same could be said for poem 47, where octosyllabic lines are grouped in stanzas eight lines long. The *envoi*, borrowed from the *chanson royal*, finds its place here (cf. notes to poems 20 and 45).

    Deschamps displays a great sense of humour in ballades such as this and takes delight in portraying himself as a testy old man and even in self-ridicule to gain sympathy (cf. poem 49, 'Eustaces, qui a la teste tendre').

47 This octosyllabic ballade (cf. notes to poem 46) is in dialogue form and full of verve and wit. One has to imagine two young dandies from court encountering each other in a cobbled street. Again, there is an *envoi*.

48 This ballade, which was probably written in 1371, shows Deschamps in his rôle of chronicler: it celebrates two births in the royal house of France, Charles V's sons, Charles VI (born 3 December 1368) and Louis d'Orléans (born 3 March 1371). Deschamps tells the stars beneath which the princes were born and, in the *envoi*, names Louis' godfather as the famous soldier Bertrand (du Guesclin, d. 1380).

49 Deschamps, poking fun at his own feeble constitution, asks his patron, the duc d'Orléans, for permission to retain his hat while serving him in the winter months, on account of his baldness and the cold weather. A further ballade, entitled 'Lettres de Monseigneur d'Orliens par maniere de balade', contains the duke's gracious permission.

50 & 51 The two texts of this double ballade (cf. notes to poems 17 and 18) were set to music in the polytextual manner by a musician named F. Andrieu, about whom nothing else is known (the manuscript source is Chantilly, Musée Condé, 1047). The question arises, did Deschamps deliberately write these two ballades with identical structure and refrain, to be set to music in this way? The answer in this case is probably yes, for the texts are in homage to the greatest musician of the fourteenth century, Guillaume de Machaut, and lament his death in 1377. The words themselves summon all singers and instruments to weep for Machaut's death and it would have been most fitting for Deschamps to engage a musician to set his heart-felt tribute.

The opening line, 'Armes, Amours, Dames, Chevalerie', was also used by Deschamps as the refrain for his ballade 'Qui saroit bien que c'est d'Amours servir'. These words may have been a motto of the king of Aragon and a ballade with this refrain was addressed to that monarch in 1388 by Trebor (cf. notes to poem 38). Froissart adapted the line to 'D'Armes, d'Amours et de Moralité' in a ballade refrain in the *Trésor amoureux* (poem 38) and, what is more, a Catalan song addressed to Gaston Phébus by Peyre de Rius (who was in the service of the court of Aragon but is recorded in 1375, 1380 and 1381 as 'trobador de danses' and 'trobador de canços' at the court of the count of Foix) commences: 'Armes, Amors et Cassa'.

52 Deschamps, presumably writing in 1377 or shortly afterwards, here addresses a ballade to Machaut's former inspiration, the lady Péronne (cf. poem 21). Deschamps makes obvious reference to his own lament on Machaut's death (cf. poems 50 and 51) by the line 'Tous instrumens l'ont complaint et plouré', and line 5 tells us that he owed more than an artistic debt to Machaut 'Qui m'a nourry et fait maintes douçours'. The theme of the poem, that Péronne could honour Machaut's memory in no better way than by allowing Deschamps in turn to become her 'loyal ami', may seem a little surprising, but should surely be read simply as an elegant compliment on the poet's part.

53 It is the ballade form above all which Deschamps used to express his very varied inspiration. This example, full of life and curiosity, is the advice of Deschamps the experienced traveller that, no matter what the hardships of journeying, there is little profit to be gained in never venturing from home, for '*Il ne scet rien qui ne va hors*'. The poem's date is *c.* 1385.

54 It was once strongly believed that the world would come to an end with the year 1000. As the year 1400 approached the same belief gained ground, especially since so many moralisers blamed the troubled state of France, torn between civil strife and the One Hundred Years War, on the corruption of the times and threatened heavenly retribution. Deschamps wrote this ballade about 1394 and catches this spirit brilliantly with his images of sterility and the mood he conveys of anguish and confusion. He plays the moraliser himself and does not omit to urge repentance before it is too late.

55 This ballade in twelve-line stanzas, written in 1396, shows Deschamps in bitter mood: faithful servant of the royal house of France and recorder of the glorious deeds of the realm for thirty-two years, he had nevertheless received no invitation to the marriage ceremonies between Isabelle, daughter of Charles VI, and Richard of England. The poet, full of disappointment and frustration, wishes to end his 'livre de memoire': he lists some of the most important events he has witnessed—the reign of Charles V, Bertrand de Guesclin's victories over the English and his burial at St Denis, the birth of Charles VI and his brother Louis (cf. poem 48), the popular uprisings and disturbances in France, the coronation of Charles VI at Reims and the subsequent events of his reign. All this Deschamps had faithfully recorded and now he is excluded from a royal wedding! We can only read as bitterly ironical the refrain '*Noble chose est de bon renom acquerre*'.

56 Unsanitary conditions in mediaeval townships did nothing to hinder the spread of plague and epidemics were frequent. In 1399 Deschamps was in Paris at the time of such an epidemic and this ballade, which is full of good humour, sets out his very practical recommendations in order to avoid the plague.

57 This ballade with *envoi* was written about 1403 in reply to an *Épître* from Deschamps' young contemporary, Christine de Pisan. In 1403 Deschamps was fifty-seven and Christine de Pisan was about forty. Deschamps is most complimentary to Christine and he clearly esteems her gifts very highly.

58 Deschamps chooses the octosyllabic line for his famous ballade on old age. Again he takes pleasure in ridiculing himself, but with extreme perceptiveness notes all the unpleasant characteristics of senility, both physical and psychological. The point of the poem comes in the *envoi*: people who should love and esteem the aged poet are

already wishing him out of the way and dead. Deschamps is here protesting against the poor treatment he is known to have received sometimes at court, especially from the younger members of the court circle. The poem was written about 1406, when Deschamps was sixty years old and, indeed, on the point of death.

59 This is an excellent *chanson royal* with refrain, written about 1384, on the *memento mori* or *ubi sunt* theme: where are the great figures of the past? where are Sampson, Solomon, Hippocratus, Plato, Orpheus, Ptolemy? where are the Romans? where are the ancient heroes of France and where are the saints? all are returned to dust and we are all equal before Death—'*Tuit y mourront, et li fol et li saige*'. We should turn from vice and sin and meet Death with a pure heart. This type of moralising greatly preoccupied Deschamps in his declining years (cf. poem 54) and he also wrote a number of poems on religious themes, including ballades to the Virgin Mary.

The theme knew widespread popularity, especially in the fifteenth century (perhaps in conjunction with the Dance of Death), and François Villon gives an effective version of it in his *Ballade des dames du temps jadis*.

60 Deschamps here gives in a virelai a delightful portrait of a young girl admiring her own beauty. The shorter, seven-syllable lines slip past with tremendous verve and humour, and the psychological observation is very acute.

Formally this is something of a curiosity: it is the virelai reduced to the simplest possible form. Historically speaking, if this were still set to music, it would have only *one* line of text to each music section. The refrain line, however, alternates between two versions, '*Sui je, sui je, sui je belle?*' and '*Dittes moy se je suis belle*'. Moreover, because of the extreme brevity of the scheme (it is a complete virelai form in only five lines), the text is then extended greatly to a total length of forty-five lines, the constantly recurring but alternating refrains lending an extra air of coquetry to the girl's self-admiration.

CHRISTINE DE PISAN

61 An early ballade with *envoi* in which Christine praises the kindness and gentle devotion of her husband (*Balades de divers propos* B XXVI).

62 This ballade with *envoi*, B VI of the *Cent Ballades,* in which Christine de Pisan bitterly laments her husband's death (1389), is known in a musical setting by Binchois (q.v. poem 83). Binchois' setting has to omit the *envoi*, of course, since there is no place for it in the musical structure (cf. notes to poems 20 and 45). The major poets of the late fourteenth and early fifteenth centuries were no longer masters of the musical art, but there was nothing to stop musicians from setting their verses for them on occasion (cf. poems 50 and 51). A number of examples of this practice are known from the late middle ages and, indeed, from earlier times.

63 In the short seven-line stanzas of this ballade with *envoi* (B XI of the *Cent Ballades*) Christine de Pisan uses a repetition technique which became especially popular— perhaps far too popular—in the fifteenth century: the opening of each line throughout a poem with an identical phrase could be a sterile exercise in unskilled hands. With Christine, however, the repetition of 'Seulete suy' hammers home the dull pain and grief of the young widow, still deep in mourning.

64 This ballade (B LXXVIII of the *Cent Ballades*) is of a very different nature from the preceding three examples, though it still has the husband as its theme. Elsewhere Christine de Pisan takes care to explain that she is virtuous and correct in her conduct and that poems such as this are nothing but a *divertissement* for courtly circles. The text takes up the old trouvère theme of the *mal mariée* with a vengeance!

65 A further ballade (B VIII of *Balades de divers propos*) on a husband and in the same vein as poem 64. The poem has to be understood as a piece of 'tongue in the cheek' writing: a vivacious young wife praises her husband to the skies—he is so kind and considerate that he lets her do whatever she wishes and even laughs when she welcomes her lover!

66 This poem (B XXXIV of *Balades de divers propos*) is notable for two features: first, Christine de Pisan writes a lover's lament from a man's point of view (cf. poem 1, where Jehan de Lescurel gives a ballade spoken by a lady). Secondly, the form is curious and shows Christine's experimental approach. Words have become com- pletely dissociated from music in the poet's mind and she feels free to reorganise the lyric forms. She has used seven-syllable lines for the body of the stanzas, something which was rare enough in the works of Machaut and his followers; but her introduction of *two* short lines of four syllables, not at the conventional 'short line point' of line 5, but as the final and penultimate, and these as a *two-line refrain*, is a serious divergence from the Ars Nova form, though they remind one of Lescurel and Acart (q.v.) at the beginning of the fourteenth century.

67 This is a ballade 'à rimes reprises' from *Le Livre du Duc des vrais Amans*. Like the preceding item, it expresses the lover's point of view. Formally it is noteworthy for its unusually short six-line stanzas and, of course, for the difficult technique of 'rimes reprises', the repetition of the rhyme at the end of one line at the opening of the next.

68 This is B IV of *Balades de pluseurs façons*, a group in which Christine de Pisan de- liberately sets out to ring the changes on traditional ballade form. This ballade, in twelve-line stanzas of lines of seven and three syllables, seems at first sight reminiscent of poems by Acart or Machaut (q.v.), but nevertheless represents a completely new departure, for its rhyme schemes could never fit into a musical setting. It was a

fundamental rule of the traditional form that lines set to the same music section had to have the same rhyme scheme; Christine's stanzas can only be split into two main divisions in this case, the final six lines being the repetition of the opening six.

69 This ballade (B XXVIII from *Cent Balades d'amant et de dame*) is similar to the preceding item in the essential binary structure of its stanzas and in the impossibility of fitting this into the traditional musical scheme. Never before had a shorter line appeared in the position of line four, for historically the repetition of the first music section always dictated an even and balanced number of lines up to this point. Again, Christine de Pisan uses a shorter line as the refrain.

70 In this, the B XLVII of *Cent Balades d'amant et de dame*, Christine again uses seven-syllable lines and a two-line refrain. The lover and the lady converse in alternate stanzas, the lady closing the conversation in the *envoi*. The situation, of the couple's grief because the lover has to depart, is very reminiscent of certain *Chansons de Croisade* in the early thirteenth century.

71 If Christine de Pisan took liberties with the traditional ballade form, her treatment of the rondeau was far more drastic. Mixed metres in rondeau settings had been known in the thirteenth and early fourteenth centuries (cf. poems 4 and 10) but were not favoured by Machaut or his followers. Here Christine chooses to use lines of seven and of three syllables. The greatest innovation, however, is her treatment of the refrain: this is given in its entirety at the outset as convention demanded (here it is six lines long), but the traditional repetition of the first half of the refrain after a matching section of new text and of the complete refrain at the close of the composition is abandoned. Instead, each time Christine gives the first line only. The traditional repetitions had been intimately tied up with the structure of the rondeau musical setting. With musical considerations removed, there was no longer a *raison d'être* for the return of so much text. This innovation causes a great deal of confusion, for it was already a normal scribal practice to give only the *incipit* of the refrain in the manu-script to indicate the full repetition. Indeed, the idea of having a shortened refrain may well have been prompted by this scribal shorthand. From the beginning of the fifteenth century it is therefore often hard to determine from the *incipit* in the manuscript whether a full refrain or the first line only was intended by the poet. Quite often the sense of the text can make this clear and all musical settings naturally involve the full repetitions of the refrain. The situation is made more difficult by the development in the fifteenth and sixteenth centuries of a deliberately short refrain line, only the first word or words of the first line being used again. Many editorial inaccuracies have resulted from misunderstanding of the nature of the refrain (cf. Villon's rondeau 'Mort, j'appelle de ta rigueur' from *Le Testament*: Longnon(ed. CFMA, 1958) prints the repetitions of the refrain simply as 'Mort?' the first time and 'Mort!' the second. There are good grounds for believing that Villon meant more than this to reoccur).

72　This rondeau, from the close of the *Livre du Duc des vrais Amans,* is similar to poem 71 in form, using mixed metres and the shortened refrain. The form is shortened further, however, after line 10, for the usual passage of new text (here to match lines 1–3) is absent. This may be due to a scribal omission, but the flow of the text from line 10 to line 11 suggests that this is the way Christine planned it.

The poem is again written from the lover's standpoint.

73　This is the shortest possible rondeau: Christine de Pisan shows her wit in this cryptic little piece with *one* syllable to each line and a shortened refrain. This is a good example of the way in which the meaning of a text can determine how much of the refrain is to reappear (cf. notes to poem 71). The last word has to be '*Dieux*' and there is no place for a further '*Est*' after that.

74　This virelai continues the tradition of the 'realistic virelai' (cf. poem 35) with its Spring setting and its bird song. Here again, though, Christine cuts out the lengthy repetitions of the refrain demanded by the conventional musical setting and each time uses the first line only (cf. notes to poem 71).

75　This virelai comes from the close of the *Livre du Duc des vrais Amans*. Like poem 74, it uses the shortened refrain.

ALAIN CHARTIER

76　A regular decasyllabic ballade in long, twelve-line stanzas. Despite his later date, Chartier is not given to experimentation or technical brilliance in the Christine de Pisan manner. The theme is that of all Chartier's lyric compositions: the lover laments his unhappy lot and unrequited passion. In this particular poem the love is unrequited because Death has stolen the lover's lady from him ('ma joie est soubz la tombe emmurée'); the poet longs to join her in the tomb.

77　A ballade with *envoi* again on the theme of unrequited love. Images of flowers and gardens were a popular device (cf. Machaut, poem 11; Froissart, poem 37) but Chartier develops his idea of a 'tree of love' with considerable skill: the plant is rooted in his heart; it only bears the fruit of woe; its leaves are of chagrin and its blossoms of grief; the tree has grown rapidly, and far around beneath its shade all joy has withered; the poet has watered it with his doleful tears but the fruit is no better for it; nevertheless he sustains his heart on this bitter fruit; if only, now that it is Spring, Love would prune away the branches of frustration and graft on a branch of pleasure ('plaisance'), joyous buds would soon appear. The *envoi* is fittingly addressed, not to the conventional *Prince*, but to 'Ma Princesce' and the refrain explains that he can neither tear this tree of love from his heart nor plant another in its place.

78 The question arises, with Chartier's rondeaux, as to whether the refrains are to reappear in their entirety or in part only (cf. notes to poem 71). Piaget is certainly incorrect when, in his edition, he omits them altogether. This rondeau, 'Triste plaisir et douleureuse joie', is known in a musical setting by Binchois (q.v. poem 83) and, because of the traditional musical structure, has to appear in its entirety; there could be no question of a shortened refrain. In our present edition this has been accepted as the pattern for Chartier's rondeaux and they are all presented with complete refrains. Chartier is, after all, completely in accord with the formal practices of the poet-musicians of his time (see poems 82–5) when he exploits the sixteen-line and twenty-one-line rondeau types. This was the pattern which dominated the fifteenth century, whereas in the fourteenth century the simple eight-line type flourished above all.

This is a typical example of the sixteen-line rondeau:

[*Music:* I   II   I   I   I   II   I   II   ]

Text: $A_{10}B_{10}B_{10}A_{10}$ $a_{10}b_{10}A_{10}B_{10}$ $a_{10}b_{10}b_{10}a_{10}$ $A_{10}B_{10}B_{10}A_{10}$

79 A sixteen-line rondeau. The poet's image is a little curious in its artificiality: he is held by the power of his lady's eyes, but these cause him grief while promising joy; one eye gives him more pain than he can endure while the other makes him live in hope! This is exactly the type of paradoxical (and, dare one say, slightly ridiculous) situation so greatly loved and exploited throughout the middle ages.

80 A twenty-one-line rondeau:

[*Music:* I   II   I   I   I   II   I   II   ]

Text: $A_{10}A_{10}B_{10}B_{10}A_{10}$ $a_{10}a_{10}b_{10}A_{10}A_{10}B_{10}$ $a_{10}a_{10}b_{10}b_{10}a_{10}$ $A_{10}A_{10}B_{10}B_{10}A_{10}$

Although this is a rondeau, the nature of its text is in keeping with that of the 'realistic virelai' (cf. poem 35). Chartier again displays exceptional ability in the development of his theme. The depiction of the bustle and agitation of people rushing to put out a fire, however, and the image of the lover's heart catching fire through its extreme ardour were by no means new (cf. also poem 88, a ballade by Charles d'Orléans).

81 A twenty-one-line rondeau in octosyllabic lines. The poet this time makes a direct complaint to his lady: she should either save him or finish him off, for because of her lack of mercy he feels close to death. The refrain hinges on another paradox: the lady is so beautiful and kind that she surely would not know how to hate and yet she shows no love.

FIFTEENTH-CENTURY LYRIC PIECES SET TO MUSIC

82 The sixteen-line and twenty-one-line rondeaux were the types favoured by fifteenth-century musician-poets and they knew a tremendous vogue. In the musical context, at least, there was a considerable swing in taste from a preference for the ballade in the mid- and late fourteenth century to the rondeau in the fifteenth century. It is curious to note that a similar change in taste took place in Italy in the Trecento. Early in the 1300s the madrigal was favoured above all, but later on the Italian ballata (similar to the French virelai in form) came to supplant it.

The Dufay example here is a twenty-one-line type in octosyllabics. The text displays humour in the worn-out old poet's declaration that if he could be young again he would win success through guile ('Je feroye fort du rusé!').

See music example no. 14.

83 Binchois, as we have already seen (poems 62 and 78), made musical settings of a number of poems by non-musician poets. The text (and music) of 'Jamais tant que je vous revoye' is his own composition, a twenty-one-line rondeau in octosyllabics.

84 This example by Grenon is a sixteen-line rondeau in decasyllabics. The lover affirms his loyalty and devotion to his lady.

85 This sixteen-line octosyllabic rondeau by J. Legrant concerns the traditional *lozengier*, here called *mesdisans*, the jealous trouble-makers who seek to spoil the course of true love.

See music example no. 15.

CHARLES D'ORLÉANS

86 This decasyllabic ballade with *envoi* by Charles d'Orléans has long stanzas of eleven lines each. Taking the traditional lover's greeting on May day as his framework, the poet expresses his sorrow in exile: Fortune, never to be relied upon, has made him spend most of his youth 'en doloreux party'.

87 A short ballade with *envoi* in octosyllabic eight-line stanzas. The poet cannot sleep at night since his heart insists on reading 'Ou rommant de Plaisant Penser', a book made up of the 'fais de ma Dame sans per'.

88 A decasyllabic ballade in nine-line stanzas, this takes up the image of the lover's heart on fire and the difficulty in extinguishing the flames. It will be remembered that this was a theme especially suitable to the fourteenth-century 'realistic virelai' but that Chartier took it up in his rondeau 'Au feu! au feu!' (poem 80). A comparison

between the Chartier and Charles d'Orléans poems is interesting: the ballade form, of course, gives Charles d'Orléans far more chance for expansion. In Chartier's rondeau the poet's heart is aflame simply with the 'ardant desir d'Amours'; with Charles d'Orléans it is the 'Ardant desir de vëoir ma maistresse'. Chartier concen/ trates more on the visual aspects of the scene: his

> Flambe, chaleur, ardeur par tout s'espart,
> Estincelles et fumée s'en part.
> Embrasé sui du feu qui croit tousjours

has no real parallel in Charles d'Orléans, who is more introspective. In the Chartier example the poet himself cries for help ('A l'aide, helas!'), whereas in Charles d'Orléans the heart itself is heard to '*crier piteusement secours*'. Charles d'Orléans' line 14 ('Au feu, au feu, courez, tous mes amis') is very similar to the opening of the Chartier poem. Both poets have tried to put the fire out, Chartier with 'Eaue de pitié, de larmes et de plours', Charles d'Orléans with 'lermes à largesse'. Chartier does not go as far as Charles d'Orléans, who asks for a mass to be said for his heart if it perishes in the flames; given the relative lengths of the two poems it might fairly be said that Chartier's rondeau is the more effective.

89 Charles d'Orléans here throws down a challenge to *Dangier*, who has caused him to stay so long in exile ('loings demourer / De la nompareille de France') and has wounded so many lovers. *Dangier* is to surrender to *Léauté* or it will be the worse for him ('vous y mourrés / Par mes mains')! The poet is clearly in bellicose mood.
   Formally, this ballade is notable for the extreme length of its stanzas, fifteen lines each, a sure sign that the verse has been liberated from the constraints of music (cf. notes to poem 11).

90 This ballade is unique in its use throughout of five/syllable lines. Charles d'Orléans is prepared to make experiments in form, though he does not make such drastic departures from tradition as Christine de Pisan. The poet here criticises those who hope for swift rewards in love:

> Car qui loyaument
> Veulent acquester
> Bon guerdonnement,
> Maint mal endurer
> Leur fault.

91 This ballade with *envoi*, in seven/line stanzas with seven syllables to the line, bring Charles d'Orléans' later preoccupation with *Nonchaloir* to the fore. *Nonchaloir* is best defined as 'a state of no longer caring to love mingled with nostalgia for past happiness, a fear of suffering anew and a desire to dwell in repose'. The word and idea of

Nonchaloir is not original in Charles d'Orléans—it is used by Machaut, for instance (e.g. poem 20, line 47)—but Charles d'Orléans takes the theme and exploits it in far greater depth than any of his predecessors. *Nonchaloir* is a departure from traditional courtliness, and it is the key attitude in the poems of Charles d'Orléans' maturity. In this poem *Nonchaloir* is seen as a medicine, a cure for '*L'amoureuse maladie*'.

92   Charles d'Orléans presided over a brilliant and flourishing *Puy* or Court of Love at Blois after his return from exile: the ancient traditions of poetic debate were fostered there, above all in the ballade and rondeau forms. At banquets minstrels sang, mystery plays were performed, and there was juggling and tableaux-vivants.

     The line 'Je meurs de soif en couste la fontaine', a typical paradox which appealed greatly to mediaeval taste, was one of many put forward for development by various poets in competition. Charles d'Orléans' elaboration of the theme seems competent enough and stands up well in comparison with the more celebrated version by François Villon, who was a visitor at Blois about 1457.

93   A twenty-one-line rondeau, called 'chanson' in the manuscript sources (see introductory note on Charles d'Orléans).

94   A sixteen-line rondeau ('chanson'), one of a group of eight on the theme of kissing which alternate in the manuscript sources with other rondeaux taking up themes elsewhere exploited in the ballades.

95   A sixteen-line rondeau ('chanson') with only four syllables to the line. Charles d'Orléans is again taking pleasure in a little restrained experimentation. Compare this with his rondeau with five syllables to the line (poem 96), his ballade with five syllables to the line (poem 90) or with Christine de Pisan's rondeau with one syllable to the line (poem 73).

96   A sixteen-line rondeau with only five syllables to the line (see notes to poem 95). The poet here declares that he would rather lose his eyes than see *Beaulté* (i.e. a beautiful woman) and fall into her power.

97   Among the secondary themes of Charles d'Orléans' poetry are those of *Fortune* and *Nature*, 'elements of non-psychic reality, which however influenced his moral and mental states' (H. Watson, in *Romanic Review*, LVI (1965)). This rondeau, presented here with shortened refrains after the manner of Christine de Pisan, is a deservedly famous and particularly delicate evocation of the coming of Spring.

98 A rondeau with shortened refrains. As age creeps upon him Charles d'Orléans progresses from *Nonchaloir* to Melancholy and, ultimately, to *Ennui*, used almost in Baudelaire's sense of Spleen. He has reached a state of psychological and sentimental inertia—the world is tired of him and he is tired of the world.

99 A rondeau with shortened refrains, basically on the twenty-one-line rondeau pattern. This is a poem of Charles d'Orléans' old age, comparable in some ways perhaps to Deschamps' ballade on senility (poem 58). Charles d'Orléans, however, concentrates less on picturesque details and more on allegorical technique, introducing the figures of *Jennesse, Viellesse, Foiblesse* and *Destresse.*

100 One of the few virelais composed by Charles d'Orléans, presented here with the final shortened refrain. There is no attempt here to exploit the complex and lengthy type of virelai with mixed metres; the poet contents himself with a very simple version of the form. Champion lists the piece in error as a rondeau in his edition.

The secondary theme of Nature is again exploited here (cf. poem 97) and the poem consists of a tirade against the inclemencies of Winter.

MUSICAL EXAMPLES

NOTE: The original manuscripts give no indication as to speed or dynamics—these are best
left to the musical sense of the performers. Nor
was there any indication of the forces involved—
the vocal lines may be doubled by suitable
instruments and the lines without text taken by
such instruments as viola, 'cello, bassoon, trom-
bone, lute or recorders. The judicious use of bell
chimes and percussion can be effective.

Music examples Nos. 1, 2, 3, 9, 12, 14, 15
are taken, by kind permission of Dr Armen
Carapetyan, from my own transcriptions in
vols. 30, 36 and 37 of the *Corpus Mensurabilis
Musicae* of the American Institute of Musicology
(1966). The remaining examples are newly
transcribed for the present publication.

JEHAN DE LESCUREL

1. BALLADE

B.N., f.fr. 146, f. 57r°

1. A - mour, vou - lés vous a - - cor - der
2. Que je mui - re pour bien a - mer? 3. Vo vou - loir

m'es - teut a - - gré - er; 4. Mou - rir ne puis plus dou - ce -

- ment. 5. Vrai - e - ment, 6. A - mours, fa - ciez vou - stre ta - lent.

Ed. Wilkins, *CMM*, vol. 30, p. 3.]

4. RONDEAU

B.N., f.fr. 146, f. 59r°

1, 5, 9. Dou - ce de - sir - ré - - e, 2, 10. Fa - ciez moi se -
4. Moult for - - ment m'a - gré - - e,
6. La dou - - ce pen - sé e 7. Qui me croist touz

- cours; 3, 11. Pour vous seuf - - fre griés dou - lours.

jours 8. En es - - pe - - rant voz dou - çours:

Ed. Wilkins, *CMM*, vol. 30, p. 16.]

1, 13. Dis tans plus qu'il ne - fau - - droit   flours   2, 14. A
9. Ne senz grie - tés, mes granz dou - - çours   10. Dès

faire un mont jus - ques és   ciex 3, 15. Man
que vous re - mir de mes   iex; 11. En

à vous sa - lus et dou - - çours 4, 16. Et
moi croit tout ain - si a - - mours 12. Loi -

Fine

veil d'a - mer moi vous doint Diex.   5. Jeune et
- aus puis par vous ai. biens tiex.   7. Ho - neur

belle et gra - ci - eu - - se,   6. En vous
et joie a - mou - reu - - se   8. Ai - ez,

|1|

|2| D.C.

ai tout mon cuer mis;
frans cuer   dous, tou - dis.

[Ed. Wilkins, *CMM*, vol. 30, p. 18.]

GUILLAUME DE MACHAUT

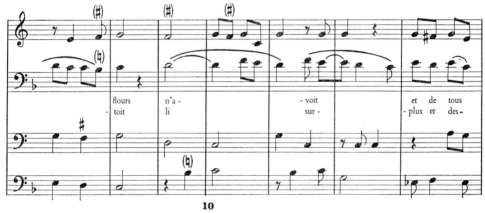

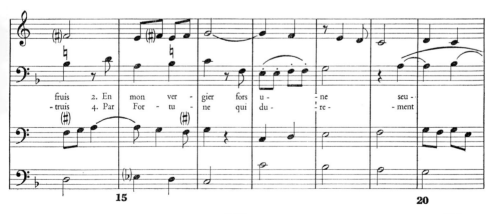

- dour. 7. Mais se cueil - lir la voy ou tres-bu - chier,

8. Autre a - -près li ja mais

a - - voir

45

55

149

[Ed. Schrade, vol. III, pp. 118–119; the Cantus only should be sung (by a soloist) and the remaini three lines taken by appropriate instruments.]

5 16. BALLADE   B.N., f.fr. 1584, f. 456v°, e

9. En   mes   lan -   - gours
12. S'en   croist   mes   plours

10. Car   d'ail -   - lours   11. N'est riens   qui
13. Tous   les   jours,   14. Quant tes   cuers

con - fort   m'a -   - maint.   ne   maint.
en   moy

[Ed. Schrade, vol. III, p. 77.]

fu - rent dig- - nes d'on-

n'ay par nul tour 6. Des yeux Ar-

45

-nour. 6. Mais quant je voy de biau - té l'um - ble flour, 7. As - se - vis

-gus ne de joi - e grin - gnour, 7. Car pour plai - sance et

50 55

sui de tout, si que, par m'a- - me,

sanz a - ÿ - de d'a- - me

60

154

65

70

75

80

[Ed. Schrade, vol. III, pp. 124–127; the cantus I and cantus II are to be sung simultaneously by two soloists, with instruments taking the lower two parts.]

B.N., f.fr. 1584, f. 475v°, etc.

1, 4, 7. Dix
3. Pris
5. Pour

et sept, cinq,
ha en moy
sa bon - té

tre -
une
que

se, qua - torse
a - mou - reuse
chas - cuns loe

et
em -
et

5

quin -
- pri -
pri -

- se
- se
- se

10

156

2, 8. M'a dou- -ce- -ment de qui
6. Et sa biau- té

bien a - mer es -
sur tou - tes a

- pris.
pris.

Ed. Schrade, vol. III, pp. 160–161.]

157

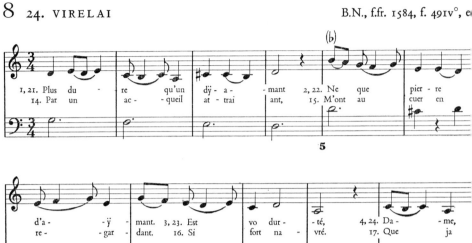

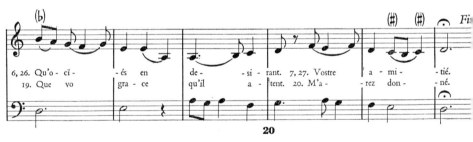

à - ne pa - mon gré, 10. Et vo sam - blant -ré, 13. En sous - ri - -ant,

Ed. Schrade, vol. III, p. 187.]

THE POST-MACHAUT GENERATION

26. BALLADE

P. DES MOLINS

B.N., nouv. acq. fr. 6771, f. 71v°

Triplum

Cantus

1. De ce que fol pen - sé sou - vent re-
3. Car par pen - ser et cuy - dier me des-

Contra-Tenor.

Tenor

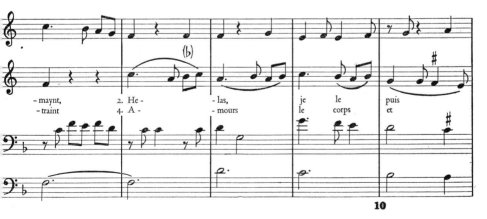

- maynt, 2. He - - las, je le puis et
- traint 4. A - - mours le corps et

159

les griefs maulz en - du - rer 6. Ce - lé - e -

P. DE CASERT

Chantilly, *Musée Condé*, MS. 1047, f. 37ᵛ

la tra- -hi et la vost es - sil - -lier; 6. For-

trait li a un jou- -el de grant pris

7. Qu'a - -voir

ne puet sanz

65

Ed. J. Wolf, *Geschichte der Mensuralnotation*, Leipzig, 1904, vols. II/III, No. 27. Note the extreme complexity of the rhythm here; this is a good example of 'Ars Subtilior' but it is somewhat misleading to fit this extremely flexible music into the straightjacket of modern bar-line divisions.]

31. BALLADE J. SENLECHES

B.N., nouv. acq. fr. 6771, f. 61v°

Ed. W. Apel, *French Secular Music of the Late Fourteenth Century*, Cambridge, Mass., 1949, No. 47.
The rhythm here is not so flamboyant as in the preceding example, but still displays a marked taste
or syncopation.]

ANON

B.N., nouv. acq. fr. 6771, f. 65v°–66r

Cantus

1, 4, 7. Pas - - se - - ro -
3. En   vous   pen -
5. Ne   quier   que

Contra-Tenor

Tenor

5

- se   de
- ser   tous
al -   - tre -

biau -   - té   pure
jours   mes   cuers
- ment   ma   vie

10

15

168

et
ne
de -

fi -
fi -
- cli -

- ne
- ne,
- ne,

2, 8. Et
6. Car

de
sans

bon -
vous

- té
n'ay

tres
bien,

dou-
jo -

[Ed. Wilkins, *CMM*, vol. 36, pp. 64–65. The upper, cantus part here is taken by a solo singer; the lower two parts are instrumental and are an extremely skilful and successful example of mensuration canon—the contra tenor plays the same notes (melodically) as the tenor but lengthens the duration value of the longer notes by one third. The shorter note values remain the same in each part, with the result that the tenor gradually moves further and further ahead of the contra tenor, which has to abandon the 'unused' notes of its part at the centre and at the close of the composition.]

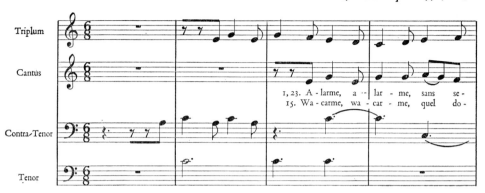

1, 23. A - larme, a - lar - me, sans se -
15. Wa - carme, wa - car - me, quel do -

- jour 2, 24. Et sans de - mour, 3, 25. Car mon las cuer si est en plour. 4, 26. A -
- lour 16. Et quel lan - gour 17. Sue - fre, da - me, pour votre a - mour. 18. Wa -

5

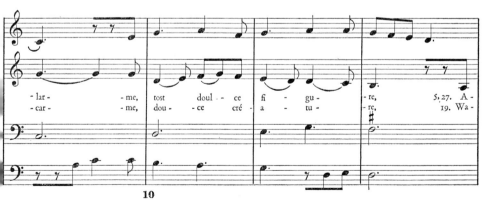

- lar - - me, tost doul - ce fi - gu - re, 5, 27. A -
- car - - me, dou - - ce cré - a - tu - re, 19. Wa -

10

15

20

Fine

[Ed. Apel, *op. cit.,* No. 72; a fairly complex and rhythmically very lively composition.]

FIFTEENTH-CENTURY LYRIC PIECES
SET TO MUSIC

14 82. RONDEAU

GUILLAUME DUFAY

B.N., nouv. acq. fr. 6771, f. 97r

plus ser - vir ne les po - vo - -ye.
-vés vous que res - pon - de - ro - -ye?

[Ed. Wilkins, *CMM*, vol. 37, pp. 10–11; a return to comparative simplicity.]

85. RONDEAU

J. LEGRANT

B.N., nouv. acq. fr. 6771, f. 95v°–96r°

Cantus

1, 7, 13. Les mes - di - sans ont
5. Pour moy des - truire et
9. On - ques de ma da -

Contra-Tenor

Tenor

fait ra - - port
metre à mort
- me con - fort

5

2, 8, 14. Aux en - vï - eux, ne sçay co -
6. Et pren - dre fin au - cu - ne -
10. Je n'eus pour vi - vre li - e -

10

[Ed. Wilkins, *CMM*, vol. 37, pp. 8–9.]

BIBLIOGRAPHY

GLOSSARY

INDEXES

BIBLIOGRAPHY

GENERAL

P. Champion, *Histoire poétique du XVe siècle*. Paris, 1923 (2 vols.). Reprinted 1966.

G. Lote, *Histoire du vers français*, vol. II. Paris, 1951.

D. Poirion, *Le poète et le prince, l'évolution du lyrisme courtois de Guillaume de Machaut à Charles d'Orléans*. Paris, 1965.

JEHAN DE LESCUREL

F. Gennrich (ed.), *Jehannot de L'Escurel: ballades, rondeaux et diz entez sus refroiz de rondeaux.* Langen bei Frankfurt, 1964. (Reprinted from the 1921–7 edition.)

A. de Montaiglon (ed.), *Chansons, ballades et rondeaux de Jehannot de Lescurel*. Paris, 1885.

N. Wilkins (ed.), *The works of Jehan de Lescurel*, vol. 30 of the *Corpus Mensurabilis Musicae* of the American Institute in Rome, 1966.

JEHAN ACART DE HESDIN

E. Hoepffner (ed.), *La prise amoureuse von Jehan Acart de Hesdin*. Dresden, 1910.

GUILLAUME DE MACHAUT

V. Chichmareff (ed.), *Guillaume de Machaut: poésies lyriques*. Paris, 1909 (2 vols.).

A. Machabey, *Guillaume de Machaut, 130?–1377*. Paris, 1955 (2 vols.).

G. Reaney, 'Guillaume de Machaut: lyric poet', in *Music and Letters*, XXXIX (Jan. 1958), 38–51.

L. Schrade (ed.), *Polyphonic music of the fourteenth century*, vol. III. Monaco, 1956.

THE POST-MACHAUT GENERATION

W. Apel, *French secular music of the late fourteenth century*. Cambridge, Mass., 1950.

G. Reaney, 'The ms. Chantilly, Musée Condé, 1047', in *Musica Disciplina*, VIII (1954), 59–113.

N. Wilkins, 'The Post-Machaut generation of poet-musicians,' in *Nottingham Mediaeval Studies*, XII, (1968), 40–84.

JEHAN FROISSART

Julia Bastin, *Froissart: chroniqueur, romancier et poète*. Brussels, 1948.

Mary Darmesteter, *Froissart*. Paris, 1894.

A. Fourrier (ed.), *Jean Froissart: l'espinette amoureuse*. Paris, 1963.

A. Scheler (ed.), *Poésies*. Brussels, 1870–72 (2 vols.).

F. K. Shears, *Froissart chronicler and poet*. London, 1930.

BIBLIOGRAPHY

LE LIVRE DES CENT BALLADES

G. Raynaud (ed.), *Les cent ballades.* Paris (SATF), 1905.

EUSTACHE DESCHAMPS

M. de Queux de Saint-Hilaire and G. Raynaud (ed.), *Oeuvres.* Paris (SATF), 1878–1903 (11 vols.).

E. Hoepffner, *Eustache Deschamps, Leben und Werke.* Strasbourg, 1904.

CHRISTINE DE PISAN

M. -J. Pinet, *Christine de Pisan (1364–1430). Étude biographique et littéraire.* Paris, 1927.

M. Roy (ed.), *Oeuvres.* Paris (SATF), 1886–96 (3 vols.).

K. Varty, *Christine de Pisan: ballades, rondeaux and virelais, an anthology.* Leicester, 1965.

ALAIN CHARTIER

P. Champion, *Histoire poétique du XVe siècle*, vol. I. Paris, 1923.

A. Piaget (ed.), '*La belle dame sans mercy' et les Poésies lyriques*, Lille–Geneva, 1949.

FIFTEENTH-CENTURY LYRIC PIECES SET TO MUSIC

Elisabeth Heldt, *Französische Virelais aus dem 15. Jahrhundert.* Halle, 1916.

J. Marix, *Les musiciens de la cour de Bourgogne au 15e siècle.* Paris, 1937.

G. Raynaud, *Rondeaux et autres poésies du XVe siècle.* Paris (SATF), 1889.

W. Rehm, *Die Chansons von Gilles Binchois.* Mainz, 1957.

N. Wilkins (ed.), *The fifteenth-century repertory contained in the Codex Reina*, vol. 37 of the *Corpus Mensurabilis Musicae* of the American Institute of Musicology in Rome, 1966.

CHARLES D'ORLÉANS

P. Champion, *Vie de Charles d'Orléans.* Paris, 1910.

P. Champion (ed.), *Poésies.* Paris, 1923–7 (2 vols.).

J. Chottel, *Le Duc Charles d'Orléans, 1394–1465, chronique d'un prince des fleurs de lys.* 1967.

S. Cigada, *L'Opera Poetica di Charles d'Orléans.* Milan, 1960.

J. Fox, *The Poetry of Charles d'Orléans*, 1968.

N. Goodrich, *Charles of Orleans, a study of themes in his French and in his English poetry.* 1967.

D. Poirion, *Le lexique de Charles d'Orléans dans les 'Ballades'.* Paris, 1967.

GLOSSARY

This glossary contains a selection of the more difficult words and expressions found in the text. Variant spellings and grammatical forms are included. The English equivalent given is the one which fits the context. The number preceding the colon refers to the poem, the number following it to the line.

The following abbreviations are used: *a.*, adjective; *adv.*, adverb; *cond.*, conditional; *conj.*, conjunction; *comp.*, comparative; *dat.*, dative; *def.*, definite; *dem.*, demonstrative; *f.*, feminine; *fut.*, future; *imp.*, imperative; *imperf.*, imperfect; *impers.*, impersonal; *ind.*, indicative; *infin.*, infinitive; *int.*, interjection; *interr.*, interrogative; *intr.*, intransitive; *m.*, masculine; *n.*, noun; *pl.*, plural; *part.*, participle; *pers.*, person; *poss.*, possessive; *pr.*, present; *prep.*, preposition; *pron.*, pronoun; *refl.*, reflexive; *s.*, singular; *sub.*, subjective; *subj.*, subjunctive; *sup.*, superlative; *tr.*, transitive; *v.*, verb.

AAGE, *n.m.s.* age; 99:4

ABAISSIÉE, *past part. f.* of *tr.v.*
ABAISSIER to cast down; 63:19

ABILLE, *3rd s.pr.ind.* of *refl.v.* ABILLER
to dress; 97:11

ABLEMENT, *adv.* ably, efficiently; 38:27

ABSTIEN, *imp. 2nd s.* of *refl.v.*
ABSTENIR to abstain; 59:45

ACHOISON, *n.f.s.* occasion, reason; 89:17

ACOINTANCE, *n.f.s.* acquaintance; 94:3

ACOLEZ, *imp. 2nd pl.* of *tr.v.* ACOLER
to embrace; 70:3

ACORDER, *infin.* of *tr.v.* to grant; 1:1

ACQUERRE, *infin.* of *tr.v.* to acquire,
win; 55:12; 55:22: ACQUIS *past part.*;
57:3

ACQUESTER, *infin.* of *tr.v.* to obtain;
90:13

ACROISTRE, *infin.* of *tr.v.* to increase;
18:3

ADEMIE, *n.f.s.* audience, hearing; 47:11

ADES, *adv.* now, at this moment; 20:20

ADEVINE, *1st s.pr.ind.* of *tr.v.* ADEVINER
to suspect; 58:12

ADROIS, *a.m.s.* skilful; 51:2

ADURÉE, *a.f.s.* harsh; 76:21

ADVIS, *n.m.s.*; FACENT SELON LEUR
ADVIS let them do as they will; 91:19

ADVOCAS, *n.m.s.* advocate; 59:27

AFAITE, *3rd s.pr.ind.* of *tr.v.* AFAITIER
to inform, prepare; 7:13

AFFAMER, *infin.* of *intr.v.* to be
famished; 81:15: AFFAME *1st s.pr.ind.*;
75:16

AFFIERE, *3rd s.pr.subj.* of *tr.v.* AFFERIR
to affect, hurt; 67:7

AFFONDE, *1st s.pr.subj.* of *intr.v.*
AFFONDER to plunge, sink; 67:16

AFFYE, *2nd s.pr.subj.* of *tr.v.* AFIER to
promise, assure; 35:6

AGAIT, *n.m.s.* watch-out, trap,
suspicion; 64:20

AGRÉER, *infin.* of *tr.v.* to accept; 1:3:
AGRÉE *3rd s.pr.ind.* (it) pleases; 4:4;
84:12

AGUS, *a.m.pl.* pointed; 58:21

AHERTE, *past part.f.* of *tr.v.* AHERDRE/
AERDRE to attach; 68:22

AIDOYE, *1st s.imperf.* of *tr.v.* AIDIER to
help; 82:7

AÏE/AŸE, *n.f.s.* help, aid; 35:26; 37:23

AIGREVIN, *n.m.s.* vinegar; 56:22

AILLOURS, *adv.* elsewhere; 80:15

AINS/ENS, *adv.* rather; 7:13; 7:17;
19:13; 42:16; 50:10; 66:23; 71:5:
AINS QUE as soon as; 61:13

AINT, see AMER

AÏR, *n.m.s.* anger; 47:12

AISE, *adv.* at ease; 89:37

AIST, *3rd s.pr.subj.* of *tr.v.* AIDIER to
help; 74:24

AJUDER, *infin.* of *v.* to help; 54:15 (help
ourselves?)

ALANGOURÉE, *a.f.s.* languid; 62:19

ALEGEZ, *2nd pl.imp.* of *tr.v.* ALEGER to
relieve, lessen; 1:16

ALEJANCE, *n.f.s.* consolation; 79:12

ALÏER, *infin.* of *refl.v.* to make an
alliance; 39:20

ALIGEMENT, *n.m.s.* relief; 15:19; 20:30

ALTREMENT, see AUTREMENT

AMAINT, *3rd s.pr.subj.* of AMENER to
bring, lead; 9:9

AMANRIR, *infin.* of *tr.v.* to lessen; 11:4

AMATIR, *infin.* of *tr.v.* to deaden; 11:6

AMENDEMENT, *n.m.s.* improvement;
77:14

AMER, (i) *infin.* of *tr.v.* to love; 81:3;
89:36: AINT *3rd s.pr.subj.*; 2:5; 9:10;
16:31: (ii) *a.m.s.* bitter; 62:12; 81:4
(bitterness); AMERE *a.f.s.*; 77:16

AMOULIE, *3rd s.pr.ind.* of *tr.v.*
AMOULÏER to soften; 35:8

AMPRAIGNE, *3rd s.pr.subj.* of *tr.v.*
AMPRENDRE/EMPRENDRE to
undertake; 46:18

ANEMI, *n.m.s.* enemy; 25:36

ANGLET, *n.m.s.* corner; 63:9

ANIENTI, *past part.* of *tr.v.* ANIENTIR
to annihilate; 25:14

ANIEUX, *a.m.s.* distressed; 74:32

ANOIE, see ENNOIE

ANQUELIE, *n.f.s.* columbine; 37:5

ANUY, see ENNUY

ÄOUR, *1st s.pr.ind.* of *tr.v.* ÄOURER to
adore; 17:21; 23:5; 25:32

APAISIÉE, *past part.f.* of *tr.v.* APAISIER
to please, satisfy; 63:11

APALIE, *past part.f.* of *tr.v.* APALIR to
turn pale; 37:15

APERTE, *a.f.s.* obvious, evident; 68:4;
68:15

APPAROIR, *infin.* of *intr.v.* to appear;
44:32; 46:27

APRIS, *a.m.s.* instructed, educated; 53:32;
60:43: APRISE *a.f.s.*; 69:9

ARA, *3rd s.fut.* of *tr.v.* AVOIR to have;
60:36

ARAIN/ARRAIN, *n.m.s.* bronze; 53:28;
54:1

ARBRISSEAULX, *n.m.pl.* shrubby trees;
77:22

ARDAMMANT, *adv.* ardently; 42:30

ARDRE, *infin.* of *tr.& intr. v.* to burn;
88:13: ART *3rd s.pr.ind.*; 80:1: ARS
past part.m.; 13:6

ARGUS, *n.m.pl.* opinions; 38:25

ARMÉE, *n.f.s.* expedition; 55:9

ARNÉ, *past part.* of *tr.v.* ARNER to break
the back (of), tire out; 64:13

ARONDE, *n.f.s.* swallow; 17:20; 36:16

ARPLES, *n.f.pl.* harps; 51:15

ARRACIER, *infin.* of *tr.v.* to tear out;
77:10

ARROUSÉ, *past part.* of *tr.v.* ARROUSER
to water; 77:11

ARS, ART, see ARDRE

ASEÜRÉE, *past part.f.* of *tr.v.* ASEÜRER
to assure; 84:5

ASPRE, *a.m.s.* harsh, bitter; 62:18: *a.f.s.*;
78:2

ASPRELLE, *n.f.s.* horsetail (botanical);
37:21

ASPREMENT, *adv.* violently; 15:27

ASSAILLIR, *infin.* of *tr.v.* to assault;
86:14: ASSAULT *3rd s.pr.ind.*; 77:33:
ASSAILLY *past part.*; 88:2

ASSAULT, see ASSAILLIR

ASSAULX/ASSAULZ, *n.m.pl.* assaults,
attacks; 43:17; 76:2

ASSENT, *3rd s.pr.ind.* of *refl.v.* ASSENTIR
to assent, agree; 15:35: ASSENTI *1st
s.past def.*; 6:6

ASSERRAY, *1st s.fut.* of *tr.v.* ASSEOIR to
set down, throw (dice); 92:24

ASSÉS, *adv.* greatly, very much; 50:13

ASSEVIS, *past part.* of *tr.v.* ASSEVIR to
finish; 18:7

ASSOUVIE, *past part.f.* of *tr.v.* ASSOUVIR
to satiate, complete; 76:34

ATAINT, see ATTAINDRE

ATENS, *1st s.pr.ind.* of *tr.v.* ATENDRE to
await; 92:11

ATIRE, *3rd s.pr.ind.* of *refl.v.* ATIRER to
attract, draw close; 45:12

ATOUR, *n.m.s.* preparation, dressing; 74:8

ATOURNÉ, *past part.* of *tr.v.* ATOURNER
to dress, adorn; 72:3

ATRAIANCE, *n.f.s.* attraction; 8:1

ATRAIRE, *infin.* of *tr.v.* to attract; 8:2:
ATRAIS *past part.*; 7:4

ATRAITE, *n.f.s.* attraction; 7:6

ATTAINDRE, *infin.* of *tr.v.* to affect,
reach; 71:7: ATAINT *past part.*; 2:10:
ATAINT *3rd s.pr.ind.*; 16:15

ATTRAIANT, *a.m.s.* attractive; 24:14

AUCQUES, *adv.* almost; 70:12

AUCUNEMENT, *adv.* in a certain way;
85:6

AUMOSNE, *n.f.s.* alms; 55:21; 99:5

AUTEL, *adv.* similarly, the same, 52:13

AUTREMENT/ALTREMENT, *adv.*
otherwise; 32:5; 40:26; 62:26; 76:7;
83:8; 84:6; 89:28

AUTRESSI, *adv.* also, as well; 42:26

AVANTAGE, *3rd s.pr.ind.* of *tr.v.*

AVANTAGER to benefit, bring advantage; 30:21

AVENROYE, *1st s.condit.* of *intr.v.*
AVENIR to arrive, happen; 30:15:
AVIENGNE *3rd s.pr.subj.*; 46:10

AVEUC, *prep.* with; 20:20

AVIS: CE M'EST AVIS/IL M'EST AVIS
it seems to me; 20:12; 42:31

AVISE, *3rd s.pr.ind.* of *tr.v.* AVISER to
look at, scrutinise; 28:13, 69:27:
AVISE *1st s.pr.ind.* (to advise); 28:20:
AVISON *1st pl.pr.ind.*; 59:31

AVOYE, *1st s.pr.subj.* of *tr.v.* AVOÏER to
set on (the path); 67:19: *3rd s.pr.subj.*;
68:30

AŸE, see AÏE

AŸMANT: PIERRE D'AŸMANT
lodestone; 24:2

AYMI, *int.* woe is me; 25:38: AY MI;
51:14

BABOÏN, *n.m.s.* baboon; 64:16

BAIL, *n.m.s.* tutelage, guardianship (of
regents); 55:30

BAILLER, *infin.* of *tr.v.* to give, hand out;
59:49: BAILLE *3rd s.pr.subj.*; 43:25

BAILLI, *n.m.s.* bailiff, magistrate; 50:18

BAILLIE, *n.f.s.* power, domination;
35:24

BALER, *infin.* of *tr.v.* to take pleasure
in; 58:27

BASTON, *n.m.s.* stick; 59:54

BAUDOUR, *n.f.s.* pleasure, delight; 18:21;
74:7

BAUME, *n.f.s.* balm; 23:2

BENIGNEMENT, *adv.* with pleasure;
57:26

BERNAGE, *n.m.s.* valour; 59:18

BESTE, *n.f.s.* beast; 97:5

BESTOURNÉ, *past part.* of *tr.v.*
BESTOURNER to upset, confuse; 72:8

BIAUTÉ, *n.f.s.* beauty, good looks; 17:1

BIAU, *a.m.s.* beautiful, handsome; 84:10;
  BIAUX *a.m.pl.*; 66:19; 60:23
BIS, *a.m.pl.* dark; 60:27
BLASMER, *infin.* of *tr.v.* to blame; 89:21
BLECIER, *infin.* of *tr.v.* to wound; 77:18
BLEMIE, *a.f.s.* pale; 70:13
BOINS, *a.m.pl.* good; 6:22
BOSSUS, *a.m.s.* hunchbacked; 58:1
BOURGOIS, *n.m.pl.* burghers; 50:12
BOURJONS, *n.m.pl.* buds, shoots; 77:27
BOUTE, *3rd s.pr.ind.* of *tr.v.* BOUTER to
  thrust, push, pour; 36:19: BOUTE *3rd
  s.pr.subj.*; 96:11: BOUTEZ *imp.2nd pl.*;
  80:12
BRANDON, *n.m.s.* burning arrow; 80:2
BREHAINGNE, *a.f.s.* sterile; 54:2
BRIEF, *a.m.s.* short; 31:4; 40:37; 55:25:
  adv. soon; 88:22: EN BRIEF briefly;
  38:14
BRIEFMENT, *adv.* quickly, soon; 1:17;
  31:13; 62:25; 83:14; 90:7
BRIQUE/BRICHE, *n.f.s.*: BAILLER LA
  BRIQUE set the trap; 59:49
BROUDERIE, *n.f.s.* embroidery; 97:3

CANELLE, *n.f.s.* cinnamon; 56:21
CAUT, see CHAUT
CELANS, *a.m.s.* secretive; 5:34
CELÉEMENT, *adv.* secretly; 20:28; 26:6
CELER/CELLER, *infin.* of *tr.v.* to hide;
  15:16; 68:39: CELLE *1st s.pr.ind.*; 89:14
CELLUI, *dem. pron.* that one; 77:10
CERTIFFIE, *1st s.pr.ind.* of *tr.v.*
  CERTIFFIER to assure; 47:17
CHACEZ, *imp. 2nd pl.* of *tr.v.* CHACER/
  CHASSER to chase; 80:12
CHAILLE, see CHAUT
CHANCELLE, *3rd s.pr.ind.* of *intr.v.*
  CHANCELLER to falter; 60:40
CHANUS, *a.m.s.* hoary; 58:11
CHAPEL, *n.m.s.* crown of flowers; 37:26
CHAPERON, *n.m.s.* hood; 49:10

CHAPIAUX, *n.m.pl.* hats; 60:23
CHAR, *n.f.s.* meat, flesh; 58:25: CHARS
  n.f.pl.; 56:17
CHAUSSANS, *a.m.pl.* fitted with shoes;
  60:19
CHAUT/CAUT, *3rd s.pr.ind.* of *intr.v.*
  CHALOIR to matter; 17:17; 28:12:
  CHAILLE *3rd s.pr.subj.*; 45:15; 98:4
CHEIRENT, *3rd pl.past def.* of *intr.v.*
  CHEÏR/CHËOIR to fall; 55:30
CHELEMIE, *n.f.s.* pipe; 51:19
CHETIVETEZ, *n.f.pl.* wretched state;
  46:13
CHEÜS, *past part.* of *intr.v.* CHËOIR to
  fall; 6:20
CHIEF, *n.m.s.* head; 49:6; 49:14; 49:23;
  60:7: A CHIEF VENIR to come to a
  head, get down to business; 47:15
CHIER, *a.m.s.* dear; 59:42; 64:12; 77:28:
  CHIERE (i) *a.f.s.*; 40:33; 67:1; 67:2:
  CHIERS *a.m.pl.*; 94:9
CHIERE, (ii) *adv.* dearly; 67:4 (iii) *n.f.s.*
  face; 40:32; 56:15; 62:19; 67:3; 92:19
CHIEREMENT/CHEREMENT, *adv.*
  dearly, earnestly; 86:34; 98:8
CHIERIE, *a.m.s.* precious, valued; 51:9
CHIÉS, *n.m.pl.* heads; 12:9
CHOULZ, *n.m.pl.* cabbages; 56:17
CHOYS, *n.m.s.* choice, selection (as
  supreme poet); 51:4
CÏENS, *adv.* in here; 49:21
CIEX/CIEULX, (i) *n.m.pl.* skies; 5:2;
  96:5 (ii) *dem. pron.* that; 73:5
CIPHONIE/SYPHONIE, *n.f.s.* type of
  wind instrument and also a type of
  drum; 51:17
CITEZ, *n.f.pl.* cities; 59:51
CLAMER, *infin.* of *tr.v.* to call; 25:62:
  CLAIMS *1st s.pr.ind.*; 68:13: CLAMOYE
  1st s.imperf.; 68:23
CLAMOURS, *n.f.pl.* lamentations,
  requests; 52:19

CLAVETTE, *n.f.s.* little key; 60:32

CLAVIS, *a.m.s.* tied, restrained; 30:27

CLER, *a.m.s.* clear; 5:30

CLERGIE, *n.f.s.* knowledge; 57:19

CLERS, *n.m.pl.* clerks; 50:2

CLOSE, *past part.f.* of *intr.v.* (E)CLORE to open out; 37:14

COIE/COYE, *a.f.s.* coy, shy; 2:6; 42:2; 74:4: COIS *a.m.s.* reserved; 5:22

COMBIEN, *interr. adv.* how long; 27:2

COMMANT, *n.m.s.* command; 24:34

COMMUNAULX, *a.m.pl.* in common, equally subject; 43:31

COMMUNE, *a.f.s.* ordinary, normal; 76:14

COMPAIGNE, *n.f.s.* company, band; 31:1

COMPLAINS, *1st s.pr.ind.* of *tr.v.* COMPLAINDRE to lament; 68:2: COMPLAINS/COMPLAINT *past part.*; 50:21; 52:8

COMPRAINGNE, *3rd s.pr.subj.* of *tr.v.* COMPRENDRE to include; 54:7

COMPTE, *3rd s.pr. ind.* of *tr.v.* COMPTER to reckon; 43:38

COMTE, *1st s.pr.ind.* of *intr.v.* COMPTER to possess; 76:16

CONDUIS, *n.m.pl.* protection; 11:11

CONDUIT, *n.m.s.* escort; 58:9

CONGNOYS, *1st s.pr.ind.* of *tr.v.* CONNOISTRE to know; 51:5: CONGNUY *1st s.past def.*; 57:14

CONJOÏR, *infin.* of *tr.v.* to rejoice in together; 38:5

CONJURÉE, *past part.f.* of *tr.v.* CON-JURER to implore; 76:32

CONNESTABLES, *n.m.s.* constable; 48:29

CONNINS, *n.m.pl.* wild rabbits: 56:20

CONSEULX, *n.m.pl.* pieces of advice, opinions; 44:4

CONTENANCE, *n.f.s.* show, appear-ances; 94:2

CONTENIR, *infin.* of *refl.v.* to behave; 45:19

CONTENS, (i) *n.m.s.* struggle, dispute; 55:29 (ii) *2nd s.pr.ind.* of *intr.v.* CONTENDRE to contend, fight, try; 27:8

CONTER, *infin.* of *tr.v.* to reckon up; 18:23

CONTES, *n.m.pl.* counts; 50:12; 50:21

CONTOUR, *n.m.s.* district, region; 31:13

CONTRALIER, *infin.* of *tr.v.* to go against, contradict; 43:24

CONTREFAIT, *a.m.s.* deformed; 64:6

CONVIENT/COUVIENT, *3rd s.pr.ind.* of *intr.v.* CONVENIR to be necessary; 27:7; 29:3; 51:12; 86:12

CONVOITISE, *n.f.s.* covetousness; 59:43

CORROYE, *n.f.s.* strap; 30:27

CORS, *n.m.pl.* horns; 51:15

COSTEL, *n.m.s.* side; 53:13: COSTEZ *n.m.pl.*; 86:15

COUARS, *n.m.s.* coward; 13:13

COURBES, *a.m.s.* bent; 58:1

COURCIER/COURCER, *infin.* of *tr.& intr.v.* to be angry with, reproach, grow angry; 39:13: COURCE *1st s.pr.ind.*; 92:13

COURROUCER, *infin.* of *tr.v.* to make angry; 87:7

COURROUCIÉ, *a.m.pl.* angry; 45:23: COURROCEUX, *a.m.s.*; 58:12

COURROUX, *n.m.s.* anger; 56:3; 62:12

COURS, (i) *n.m.s.* course, path; 88:25 (ii) VIENT LE COURS comes running; 16:27

COUSCHIÉ, *past part.* of *refl.v.* COUSCHIER to lie down; 87:1

COUSTE, EN COUSTE beside; 92:1

COUVERTE, (i) *a.f.s.* secretive; 68:37 (ii) *n.f.s.* shelter, hiding place; 68:38

COUVERTEMENT, *adv.* in secret; 15:18; 62:12

COUVIENT, see CONVIENT

COUVOITEUS, *a.m.s.* covetous, greedy; 58:11

COUX, *n.m.s.* cuckold; 64:15

COYE, see COIE

CRACHIER, *infin.* of *intr.v.* to spit; 64:11

CRAINT, *3rd s.pr.ind.* of *tr.v.* CRAINDRE to fear; 2:21: CRIENG *1st s.pr.ind.*; 17:22

CREMOUR, *n.f.s.* fear; 70:14

CREMUS, *past part.m.pl.* of *tr.v.* CREMIR to fear; 28:3

CREÜ, see CROIST

CREVER, *infin.* of *intr.v.* to die; 26:4

CROIST, *3rd s.pr.ind.* of *intr.v.* CROISTRE to grow; 4:7; 16:12: CRUT *3rd s.past def.*; 27:11: CREÜ *past part.*; 77:6

CUIDE, see CUYDIER

CUISINE, *n.f.s.* cooked meat; 58:25

CURE, *n.f.s.* care; 6:26; 31:4; 49:33: wish, desire 17:5; 19:38

CURER, *infin.* of *tr.v.* to care for; 7:7

CURIEUX, *a.m.s.* inquisitive, industrious; 44:26; 74:29

CUYDIER, *infin.* of *tr.v.* to think, care; 26:3: CUIDE *3rd s.pr.ind.*; 44:15: CUIDERAY *1st s.fut.*; 75:11

DART, *n.m.s.* spear, javelin; 27:21

DEBILITÉ, *n.f.s.* weakness, debility; 49:6; 49:34

DECEVANCE, *n.f.s.* deception: SANZ DECEVANCE with no deception; 2:3

DECOURANT, *a.m.s.* passing; 59:39

DECOURS, *n.m.s.* decline; 6:20; 16:40

DEDUIRE, *infin.* of *tr.v.* to delight; 65:12

DEDUIT, *n.m.s.* delight, pleasure; 12:19

DEFAUT, *n.m.s.* lack, default; 16:4

DEFFAIT, *past part.* of *tr.v.* DEFFAIRE to wear out, emaciate; 64:13

DEFFUBLER, *infin.* of *tr.v.* to uncover (oneself); 49:11

DEGREZ, *n.m.pl.* stairs; 64:19

DELAISSIÉE, *past part.f.* of *tr.v.* DELAISSIER to abandon; 63:18

DELITABLE, *a.f.s.* charming, delightful; 19:2

DELITER, *infin.* of *refl.v.* to enjoy oneself; 30:19

DELYS, *n.m.pl.* pleasure; 32:6

DEMAINE, *n.m.s.* domain, slavery; 92:17

DEMENÉS, *imp.2nd pl.* of *tr.v.* DEMENER to make, carry on; 50:7

DEMOUR, *n.m.s.* keeping, abode; 70:6

DEPORT, *n.m.s.* joy; 71:16

DEPRIE, *1st s.pr.ind.* of *tr.v.* DEPRIER to beg; 35:3

DESCONFIT, *3rd s.pr.ind.* of *tr.v.* DESCONFIRE to discomfort; 12:23

DESCONFITURE, *n.f.s.* discomfort; 25:7

DESDAING, *n.m.s.* disdain; 58:8

DESDIRE, *infin.* of *tr.v.* to contradict; 65:7

DESESPERANCE, *n.f.s.* despair; 77:29

DESIRANCE, *n.f.s.* desire; 89:39

DESISTES, *2nd pl.past def.* of *tr.v.* DIRE to say; 39:26

DESLÏEZ, *past part.pl.* of *tr.v.* DESLÏER to untie, let loose; 43:35

DESLOIAUX, *a.f.s.* disloyal, treacherous; 43:18

DESMENTIROYE, *1st s.condit.* of *tr.v.* DESMENTIR to contradict; 30:4

DESMESURÉE, *a.f.s.* unbounded; 62:1; 76:11

DESMESURÉEMENT, *adv.* excessively; 62:23

DESNATURAULX, *a.m.pl.* unnatural; 43:30

DESPIT, *n.m.s.* anger; 87:19

DESPLAISANCE, *n.f.s.* displeasure; 92:10

DESPRISE, *3rd s.pr.ind.* of *tr.v.* DES‑ PRISER to criticise; 69:13

DESRIVER, *infin.* of *refl.v.* to change one's mind; 61:23

DESSERT, *3rd s.pr.ind.* of *tr.v.* DESSER-
VIR to deserve; 64:15

DESSERTE, *n.f.s.* deserving, deserts;
68:10

DESSOUBZ, *prep.* beneath; 43:7; 76:18:
AU DESSOUBZ; 77:8

DESTAINT, *3rd s.pr.ind.* of *intr.v.*
DESTAINDRE to lose colour; 16:17

DESTOURNÉ, *past part.* of *tr.v.* DES-
TOURNER to turn aside, ward off;
72:7

DESTRAINT, *3rd s.pr.ind.* of *tr.v.*
DESTRAINDRE to squeeze; 16:20;
26:3

DESTREMPER, *infin.* of *tr.v.* to soak;
56:22

DESTRESSE, *n.f.s.* distress; 86:13

DESTROIS, *a.m.s.* distressed; 51:12

DESVER, *infin.* of *intr.v.* to lose one's
reason; 61:25

DESVOIE, *3rd s.pr.ind.* of *refl.v.*
DESVOÏER to go astray; 19:6

DETRY, *n.m.s.* delay; 35:4

DEULX, *1st s.pr.ind.* of *refl.v.* DOLOIR to
lament; 92:19

DEÜST, see DOIS

DEVERS, *prep.* towards; 79:10

DEVIE, *3rd s.pr.subj.* of *tr.v.* DEVÏER/
DESVOÏER to avoid; 56:13

DEVISE, *n.f.s.* coat of arms, motto; 28:6;
69: 26: taste, liking; 69:28

DIEX, *n.m.s.* god; 51:3

DIFFAME, *n.m.s.* dishonour; 75:25

DIT, *n.m.s.* words, sayings; 40:8; 44:33:
DIS *n.m.pl.*; 10:5; 50:10

DOBTÉS, see DOUBTER

DOINT, *3rd s.pr.subj.* of *tr.v.* DONER to
give; 5:4; 62:26

DOIS (i)/DOY, *1st s.pr. ind.* of *tr.v.*
DEVOIR to be obliged to; 50:13;
65:17; 69:10; 74:29; 86:26: DOIT
3rd s.pr.ind.; 65:18: DEÜST, *3rd*

s.imperf.subj.; 77:18; 100:11 (ii) *n.m.s.*
duct; 51:10

DOLENS/DOLENT, *a.m.s.* sad, grieving,
grievous; 16:19; 46:9; 51:14; 55:16;
62:14; 86:31; 93:15: DOLENTE
a.f.s.; 63:4; 63:11

DOLOIR, *infin.* of *tr.v.* to afflict; 44:7

DOLOREUX/DOULOREUX, *a.m.s.* sad
lamenting; 62:5; 86:17; 92:9:
a.m.pl.; 89:26

DONJON, *n.m.pl.* castle keeps; 59:51

DONQUES/DONCQUES, *conj.* therefore;
86:8; 89:22

DONT, *conj.* therefore, thus; 28:5; 71:13;
98:5

DOTRINE, *n.f.s.* doctrine, tenet; 57:3;
58:14

DOUBLER, *infin.* of *tr.v.* to redouble;
15:26; 19:19

DOUBTANCE, *n.f.s.* doubt; 14:4; 48:16;
94:11

DOUBTE, *n.f.s.* fear; 87:7; 88:5:
DOUBTES *n.f.pl.*; 53:5

DOUBTER, *infin.* of *tr.v.* to fear; 28:6:
DOUBTE *1st s.pr.ind.*; 13:15; 66:8:
DOUBTÉ *past part.m.pl.*; 28:4:
DOBTÉS *imp.2nd pl.* doubt; 84:6

DOUCHE, *a.f.s.* sweet, gentle; 32:2

DOULEREUSEMENT, *adv.* sadly, in
grief; 76:6

DOUTIEX, *a.m.s.* fearful; 5:22

DOY, see DOIS

DOYS, *n.m.pl.* fingers; 60:11

DRAME/DRAGME: PESER A DRAME
weigh things up carefully; 18:23

DROITURE, *n.f.s.* right; 6:8; 66:18

DROITURIERE, *a.m.s.* just; 40:20

DUEL/DUEIL, (i) *n.m.s.* grief, lamentation; 50:7; 62:1; 68:7; 70:10; 70:18;
72:6; 76:31; 78:12; etc.: DUELZ
n.m.pl.; 55:14; 65:14 (ii) *1st s.pr.ind.* of
refl.v. DOLOIR to lament, grieve; 72:13

DUPLICITÉ, *n.f.s.* abundance; 49:16

DURER, (i) *infin.* of *intr.v.* to continue to exist; 1:13 (ii) *n.f.s.* duration, stay; 27:19

EFFORCÉEMENT, *n.m.s.* violence, force; 76:30

EIMMI, *int.* woe is me; 19:22

EL, *pers.pron.3rd s.f.* (she/it); 76:28

ELOIGNANCE, *n.f.s.* removal at a distance; 2:1

EMBLÉ, *past part.* of *tr.v.* EMBLER to steal; 99:1

EMBRASER, *infin.* of *tr.v.* to blaze up, burn; 15:25: EMBRASÉ *past part.*; 80:8

EMBUCHEZ, *past part.pl.* of *tr.v.* EMBUCHIER to hide; 78:5

EMFERS, *n.m.s.* hell; 54:23

EMFLE, *3rd s.pr.ind.* of *tr.v.* EMFLER to puff up; 54:10

EMMURÉ, *past part.* of *tr.v.* EMMURER to immure; 76:20

EMMUTYS, *a.m.s.* muted, silent; 52:11

EMPEINÉE, *a.f.s.* busy, troubled; 30:23

EMPESCHEMENT, *n.m.s.* obstacle, obstruction; 77:24

EMPIRER/ENPIRER, *infin.* of *intr.v.* to get worse; 22:7; 29:31: EMPIRE *3rd s.pr.ind.*; 62:25

EMPLASTRE, *n.m.s.* ointment; 91:1

EMPRAINT, *3rd s.pr.ind.* of *tr.v.* EMPRAINTER/EMPREINTER/ EMPRIENTER to imprint; 16:35: EMPRIENTA *3rd s.past def.*; 6:3

EMPRISE, *n.f.s.* grip, power; 21:3; 69:3

ENBLE : TRES ENBLE furtively; 82:7

ENÇAINS, *past part.m.* of *tr.v.* ENCEIN-DRE to surround; 68:20

ENCERCHIER, *infin.* of *tr.v.* to research; 55:34

ENCHERI, *past part.* of *tr.v.* ENCHERIR to cherish; 25:58

ENCOMBRANCE, *n.f.s.* nuisance; 86:31

ENCOMBRE, *3rd s.pr.ind.* of *tr.v.* ENCOMBRER to afflict, encumber; 43:32

ENCOMBREMENT, *n.m.s.* affliction, woe; 77:4

ENFANÇON, *n.m.s.* little child; 48:17

ENFLAMBÉ, *past part.* of *tr.v.* ENFLAM-BER to set on fire; 80:3

ENFREMIE, *past part.f.* of *intr.v.* ENFREMIR to tremble; 70:21

ENGIN, *n.m.s.* treachery, trick; 69:21

ENGLOIRE, *a.f.s.* inglorious; 55:25

ENGLOUTIR, *infin.* of *tr.v.* to swallow up; 11:18

ENGOISSE, *n.f.s.* agony, anguish; 62:4; 62:11

ENGRANS, *a.m.s.* desirous; 55:5

ENNOIE/ANOIE, *3rd s.pr.ind.impers.* of *tr.v.* ENNOÏER to cause grief, annoyance; 40:14; 83:7: ANOIE/ ENNUYE *3rd s.pr.ind.*; 42:5; 76:17: ENNUYÉ *past part.* bored; 98:1

ENNUY/ANUY, *n.m.s.* distress; 47:7; 57:24; 62:17; 77:4; 89:35; 98:6 (boredom)

ENPIRER, see EMPIRER

ENQUERRE, *infin.* of *tr.v.* to seek, inquire; 44:21; 55:34: ENQUEURT *3rd s.pr.ind.*; 28:18: ENQUISE *past part.f.*; 69:22: ENQUERONS *imp. 1st pl.*; 99:8

ENS, see AINS

ENSAINT, *3rd s.pr.ind.* of *tr.v.* ENSAIN-DRE/ENCEINDRE to surround; 16:29

ENSEIGNE, *n.f.s.* battle cry; 54:21

ENSERRÉE, *past part.f.* of *tr.v.* ENSER-RER to enclose; 62:11; 63:13

ENTAME, *3rd s.pr.ind.* of *tr.v.* ENTAMER to injure, cut into; 75:5

ENTENCION, *n.f.s.* intent; 89:19

ENTENTE, *n.f.s.* intention; 75:8

ENTESTEZ, *a.m.s.* firm, resolute; 46:11

ENVIX, *adv.* with pain, in spite of one-self; 58:16

ENVOISEÜRE, *n.f.s.* happiness; 19:24

EPISTRES, *n.f.pl.* epistles, letters; 57:5: ESPISTRE *n.f.s.*; 57:25

ERMINE, *n.f.s.* ermine fur; 59:29: ERMINES *n.f.pl.*; 53:25

ERPENT, *n.m.s.* league; 12:3

ERRATIQUE, *a.m.s.* transitory; 59:39

ES, *contraction of* EN LES; 77:22, etc.

ESBAHIR, *infin.* of *tr.v.* to astound; 47:10: ESBAŸS *1st s.pr.ind.*; 92:16: ESBAÏS/ESBAHIS *past part.*; 53:14; 75:21

ESBATEMENT, *n.m.s.* pleasure, delight; 65:9; 83:3: ESBATEMENTS *n.m.pl.*; 42:12

ESCART: CHASSEZ À L'ESCART chase away; 80:12

ESCHARS, *a.m.s.* miserly; 58:12

ESCLARCIST, *3rd s.pr.ind.* of *tr.v.* ESCLARCIR to light up; 37:20

ESCONDIRE, (i) *infin.* of *tr.v.* to refuse, deny; 45:15: ESCONDIT *3rd s.pr.ind.*; 12:7 (ii) *n.m.s.* refusal; 66:8

ESCORCHIER, *infin.* of *tr.v.* to flay; 64:2

ESCOUTER, *infin.* of *tr.v.* to listen to; 87:5

ESCRIPRE/ESCRIRE, *infin.* of *tr.v.* to write; 46:16; 55:35; 66:10: ESCRIPT *past part.m.*; 55:2; 57:7; 87:9: ESCRIPTE *past part.f.*; 37:16: ESCRIVEZ *imp. 2nd pl.*; 86:35

ESGARÉE, *a.f.s.* lost, distraught; 63:6

ESJOÏR, *infin.* of *tr.& refl.v.* to gladden, be glad; 38:4; 83:5: ESJOÏS *1st s.pr.ind.*; 92:13: ESJOIE/ESJOYE *3rd s.pr.ind.*; 40:24; 68:18: ESJOŸ *past part.*; 25:44

ESLIRE, *infin.* of *tr.v.* to choose; 33:6; 45:22; 65:13

ESLONGIER, *infin.* of *tr.v.* to remove at a distance; 18:20: *refl.v.* to go away; 86:30

ESPACE/ESPASSE, *n.m.s.* time, interval; 38:23; 49:4

ESPANIE, *past part.f.* of *intr.v.* ESPANIR to blossom forth; 37:14

ESPARGNIER, *infin.* of *tr.v.* to save, spare; 76:29; 93:8

ESPART, *3rd s.pr.ind.* of *refl.v.* ESPARDRE to spread; 80:6

ESPASSE, see ESPACE

ESPIER, *infin.* of *tr.v.* to spy; 91:9

ESPINGLETTE, *n.f.s.* little pin, broach; 60:24

ESPITRE, see EPISTRES

ESPLOITTIEZ, *imp. 2nd pl.* of *intr.v.* ESPLOITIER to act; 45:17

ESPLOURÉE, *a.f.s.* tearful; 63:20

ESPRENT, *3rd s.pr.ind.* of *tr.v.* ESPRENDRE to enflame, overcome; 15:8: ESPRIS *past part.m.*; 21:2; 84:11: ESPRISE *past part.f.*; 69:14

ESPRISIER, *infin.* of *tr.v.* to value, esteem; 40:5

ESPROUVER, *infin.* of *tr.v.* to test; 90:26

ESSAUCIER, see EXAUCIER

ESSE, *contraction of* EST CE is it?; 96:12

ESSERTE, *3rd s.pr.ind.* of *refl.v.* ESSERTER to give onself entirely; 68:33

ESSIL, *n.m.s.* exile; 100:11

ESSILLIER, *infin.* of *tr.v.* to exile; 29:5

ESTAIN, *n.m.s.* tin; 53:27

ESTAINDRE, *infin.* of *tr.& intr.v.* to grow weak, fade out, put out; 71:14; 88:11: ESTAINT *3rd s.pr.ind.*; 16:21: ESTAINT *past part.m.*; 88:6; 88:13: ESTAINTE *past part.f.*; 40:22

ESTAT, *n.m.s.* state, condition; 49:8: ESTAS *n.m.pl.*; 39:18; 40:26; 53:16

ESTÉ, *n.m.s.* summer; 100:2; 100:5

ESTEUT, see ESTUET

ESTINCELLES, *n.f.pl.* sparks; 80:7

ESTRACE, *n.f.s.* race; 38:1

ESTRAINDRE, *infin.* of *tr.v.* to grip, clasp; 71:14: ESTRAINT *3rd s.pr.ind.*; 16:19; 43:36

ESTRAIS, *past part.* of *tr.v.* ESTRAIRE to extract, obtain; 7:25

ESTRANGEMENT, *adv.* strangely; 90:1

ESTRE, *n.m.s.* place; 63:15

ESTUET/ESTEUT, *3rd s.pr.ind.* of *impers.v.* ESTOVOIR to be necessary; 1:3; 1:7; 26:5

ESTUVES, *n.f.pl.* public baths; 56:13

EUR, *n.m.s.* luck, fortune; 92:11

EURE, *n.f.s.* hour; 31:6

EÜREUX, *a.m.s.* happy; 44:33

EUVRE, *n.f.s.* occupation; 76:14

EXAUCIER/ESSAUCIER, *infin.* of *tr.v.* to exalt; 38:1; 39:28; 40:6: EXAUCIÉS *past part.m.s.*; 13:19

FACE, (i) *1st s.pr.subj.* of *tr.v.* FERE to do, make; 20:41; 44:4; 46:16; 49:12; 56:11; 59:32; 64:15; 65:14: FACENT *3rd pl.pr.subj.*; 91:19 (ii) *n.f.s.* phase; 48:12

FAÇON, *n.f.s.* face, appearance; 18:9

FACONDE, *n.f.s.* loquacity; 17:2; 36:9

FAIÉE, *a.f.s.* enchanted; 92:6

FAILLE, (i) *n.f.s.* fail, doubt; 43:10 (ii) see FAILLIR

FAILLIR, *infin.* of *intr.v.* to fail, to have to; 86:3; 92:18: FAIL *1st s.pr.ind.*; 67:7; 75:10: FAULT *3rd s.pr.ind.*; 43:14: FAILLE *3rd s.pr.subj.*; 43:20: FAILLIZ *past part.*; 46:3

FAILLIS, *a.m.s.* weak, faint; 10:3

FAILLIZ, see FAILLIR

FAINDRE, *infin.* of *tr.& refl.v.* to hesitate, weaken; 71:11: FAINT *3rd s.pr.ind.*; 16:30: FAINGNE *3rd s.pr.subj.*; 31:15

FAINS, *a.m.pl.* faint, weak; 68:32

FAINT, (i) see FAINDRE (ii) *a.m.s.* cowardly, faint-hearted; 2:18; 88:17

FAIS/FAIT, *n.m.s.* deed, undertaking; 7:11; 92:22: FAIS *n.m.pl.* deeds; 10:6; 87:10: A FAIS as a burden; 7:12

FAISEUR, *n.m.s.* writer, poet; 52:3: FAYSEURS *n.m.pl.*; 50:2; 51:5

FAITIZ, *a.m.s.* elegant, pretty; 5:18

FAME, *n.f.s.* fame, renown; 28:18

FAULT, see FAILLIR

FAULTE, *n.f.s.* lack; 54:14: A FAULTE in default, in error; 72:1

FAULX, (i) *a.m.s.* false; 89:40: FAULSE *a.f.s.*; 89:32 (ii) *n.m.s.* waist; 60:12

FAUSSER, *infin.* of *intr.v.* to be deceitful: SANZ FAUSSER without deception; 1:8; 20:38

FAYSEURS, see FAISEUR

FEL, (i) *a.m.s.* wicked, vile; 12:6 (ii) *n.m.s.* wickedness; 27:13

FELON, *a.m.s.* wicked; 89:34

FERME, *a.f.s.* certain; 84:5

FESTIER, *infin.* of *tr.v.* to entertain; 94:12

FÏABLEMENT, *adv.* faithfully; 38:26

FIE/FYE, *n.f.s.* time, occasion; 47:27; 57:7

FIERE, (i) *3rd s.pr.subj.* of *tr.v.* FERIR to strike; 59:55; 67:8: FIERT *3rd s.pr.ind.*; 67:17 (ii) *a.f.s.* proud, haughty; 67:15

FIGURÉ, *past part.* of *tr.v.* FIGURER to shape; 84:10

FINER, *infin.* of *tr.v.* to end, finish; 15:21: FINE *3rd s.pr.ind.*; 32:3

FLAIRANS, *pr.part.m.pl.* of *intr.v.* FLAIRER to stench, smell; 58:22

FLAMBE, *n.f.s.* flame; 80:6

FLANS, *n.m.pl.* womb, entrails; 33:1

FLATER, *infin.* of *tr.v.* to flatter; 100:12

FLESCHE, *n.f.s.* arrow; 12:2

FLEUSTES, *n.f.pl.* flageolets; 51:19

FLUE ,*1st s.pr.ind.* of *intr.v.* FLUER to run; 58:4

FLUNS, *n.m.s.* river; 17:13

FOIBLES, *a.m.pl.* feeble; 58:21

FOIBLESSE, *n.f.s.* weakness, feebleness; 99:10

FONDRE, *intr.v.* to collapse, fall; 43:20: FONT *3rd s.pr.ind.*; 40:15: FONDE *3rd s.pr.subj.*; 67:9; 67:17

FONS, *n.m.s.* fount; 51:9

FORMENT, *adv.* strongly; 4:4

FORS, *adv.& prep.* except; 54:6; 59:13; 65:9; 93:7

FORSENNEMENT, *n.m.s.* madness, delirium; 62:2

FORT, (i) *adv.* greatly; 58:33 (ii): AU FORT what is more; 91:18

FORTRAIT, *past part.* of *tr.v.* FORT-RAIRE to deprive; 29:6

FOULZ, *a.m.s.* mad, silly; 49:25

FOURREZ, *a.m.pl.* furred, fur-lined; 60:22

FOY, *n.f.s.* faith; 67:14

FRANS, *a.m.s.* noble; 5:8: FRANCHE *a.f.s.*; 6:19

FRECHE, *n.f.s.*; EN FRECHE fallow; 77:17

FREMY, *1st s.pr.ind.* of *intr.v.* FREMÏER to tremble; 25:37

FRESQUE, *a.f.s.* fresh; 37:11

FRIQUE, *a.f.s.* elegant; 59:29

FROIT, *n.m.s.* cold, chill; 92:2

FRONT, *n.m.s.* forehead; 60:3

FUEILLES, *n.f.pl.* leaves; 77:4; 77:21

FUMÉE, *n.f.s.* anger; 30:1; 30:3; 30:4; 30:12; 30:17; 30:30

FUMER, *infin.* of *intr.v.* to be angry; 30:2; 30:6; 30:8; 30:16: FUME *1st s.pr.ind.*; 30:7; 30:11; 30:28: FUME *1st s.pr.subj.*; 30:13: FUMOYE *1st s.imperf.*; 30:2: FUMERAY *1st s.fut.*; 30:9:

FUMEROYE *1st s.condit.*; 30:5: FUMÉ *past part.*; 30:10: FUMANT *pr.part.*; 30:14; 30:16; 30:19; 30:20: FUMA *3rd s.past def.*; 30:26

FUMEUX, *a.m.s.* angry; 30:1; 30:20

FYE, see FIE

GAGE, *n.m.s.*: DE GAGE JE VOUS APPELLE I challenge you to combat; 89:29

GAINGNE, *1st s.pr.ind.* of *tr.v.* GAIGNER to gain; 92:8

GAIRES, *adv.* scarcely, hardly; 77:14

GAMBES, *n.f.pl.* legs; 60:16

GARIR, *infin.* of *tr.& intr.v.* to cure; 16:25; 17:14; 62:6; 62:22: GARIST *3rd s.pr.ind.*; 13:23: GARI *past part.*; 25:64: GARIS *past part.pl.*; 53:22

GART/GARD, *3rd s.pr.ind.* of *tr.v.* GARDER to protect; 80:5; 96:9

GASTER, *infin.* of *tr.v.* to spoil; 27:8: GASTÉS *past part.m.s.*; 11:3

GELLE, *3rd s.pr.subj.* of *intr.v.* GELLER to freeze; 37:10

GENT, (i) *n.f.s.* people; 1:10; 27:3 (ii) *a.m.s.* beautiful, handsome; 15:7; 20:12; 27:6: GENTE *a.f.s.*; 66:4; 75:10

GETEROIT, see GIETTE

GIETTE, *1st s.pr.ind.* of *tr.v.* GETER/ GIETTER to throw; 89:1: GETEROIT *3rd s.condit.*; 77:27

GINGEMBRE, *n.m.s.* ginger; 56:21

GISIÉS, *2nd pl.pr.ind.* of *intr.v.* GESIR to lie; 51:13

GLACE, (i) *3rd s.pr.ind.* of *intr.v.* GLACIER to slide, slip; 49:14 (ii) *n.f.s.* ice; 49:15

GLAIVES, *n.m.s.* death-cry; 54:22

GLAY, *n.m.s.* Iris; 37:4

GOUSTER, *infin.* of *tr.v.* to taste, savour; 15:33

GOUTE/GOUTTE, (i) *n.f.s.* gout; 13:8; 64:6: GOUTTE (ii): NE GOUTTE not at all; 96:2

GOUVERNEMENT, *n.m.s.* conduct, behaviour; 65:19

GRAINDRE, *comp.a.s.(cas sujet)* greater; 71:5: GRINGNOUR *comp.a.s.(cas régime)*; 17:5: GRINGNOURS *comp.a.pl.*; 16:37

GRAS, *adv.* scot free, completely; 45:1

GRÉ, *n.m.s.* consent, pleasure; 6:16; 24:9; 41:2; 52:17

GREGEOIS, *a.m.s.* Greek; 88:12

GRESILLE, *3rd s.pr.subj.* of *intr.v.* GRESILLER to sleet; 37:10

GRESLES, *a.m.pl.* slender; 60:11: GRESLETTE *a.f.s.* diminutive; 60:12

GREVER, *infin.* of *tr.v.* to wound, injure; 20:31; 30:9; 61:12; 87:18; 89:10: GREVEZ *2nd pl.pr.ind.*; 81:6

GREZIL, *n.m.s.* sleet; 100:10

GRIEF, (i) *n.m.s.* woe, grief; 2:17 (ii) *a.m.s.* painful, grievous; 62:2; 62:20; 66:5: GRIEF *a.f.s.*; 34:13; 34:21; 57:29; 66:12: GRIEFS *a.m.pl.*; 26:5

GRIETÉ/GRIEFTÉ, *n.f.s.* distress; 19:41; 24:49; 41:4: GRIETÉS *pl.*; 5:9

GRINGNOUR, see GRAINDRE

GRIS, *n.m.pl.* grey furs; 53:25; 60:22

GRUMELER, *infin.* of *intr.v.* to grumble; 58:17

GUERDONNEMENT, *n.m.s.* reward; 90:14

GUISE, *n.f.s.* manner, way; 69:23

GUISTERNES, *n.f.pl.* citterns; 51:19

HA, *3rd s.pr.ind.* of *tr.v.* AVOIR to have; 21:3; 25:55: OT *3rd s.past def.*; 70:10: ORENT *3rd pl.past def.*; 79:1

HABIS, (i) *n.m.pl.* clothes; 60:19 (ii) *n.m.pl.* habits, customs; 53:15

HABONDANCE, *n.f.s.* abundance; 57:8; 94:6

HAIRE, *n.f.s.* misery, affliction; 41:4

HAÏS, see HAŸR

HARDEMENT, *n.m.s.* courage; 28:3

HARDIMENT, *adv.* boldly; 47:22

HARDIS, *a.m.s.* brave, bold; 28:11; 60:34

HAROU, *int.* help!; 47:10

HART, *n.f.s.* noose; 64:5

HASART, *n.m.s.* hasard (winning number in a dice game): SUR UNG HASARD J'ASSERRAY I will toss up (for them); 92:24

HAULT, *a.m.s.* high; 59:53; 59:55; 88:23: *adv.* high; 60:10

HAYNEUSE, *a.f.s.* hateful; 27:3

HAŸR/HAÏR, *infin.* of *tr.v.* to hate; 81:2: HÉ *1st s.pr.ind.*; 24:52; 64:13; 88:16: HAÏS *past part.*; 75:11

HÉ (i) see HAŸR (ii) *int.* ha! well! I say!; 64:17; 75:15

HELIE, *a.f.s.* Helicon; 51:9

HERBERGE, *n.f.s.* shelter; 33:6

HERPES, *n.f.pl.* harps.; 51:19

HOIRS, *n.m.pl.* heirs; 59:37

HOMS, *n.m.s.* man; 59:45

HONNIR, *infin.* of *tr.v.* to shame; 20:16

HOSTEL, *n.m.s.* lodging, dwelling; 46:17

HUI/UI, *adv.* today; 54:8; 54:17; 98:3

HUIS, *n.m.s.* door; 63:8

HUMER, *infin.* of *tr.v.* to suck, sip; 58:29

IEX/YEX, *n.m.pl.* eyes; 5:10; 20:23

INIQUE, *a.m.s.* iniquitous; 55:30: *a.f.s.*; 59:9

IRE/YRE, *n.f.s.* anger; 65:4; 70:19

ISNEL, *a.m.s.* swift; 27:6

JA, *adv.* now; 54:21; 58:6; 69:5

JALOUS, *n.m.pl.* jealous people; 95:9

JAME, *n.f.s.* gem; 36:13

JARGON, *n.m.s.* tongue, language; 97:6

JENNES, *a.m.pl.* youthful; 99:13

JENNESSE, see JONESSE

JEUN, *n.m.s.* fast; 56:9: JEUSNES *n.m.pl.*; 58:27

JOENNES, *n.m.pl.* young people; 74:18

JOÏR, *infin.* of *intr.v.* to enjoy; 38:2; 47:23

JOLIVETÉ, *n.f.s.* pleasure; 59:53

JONESSE/JENNESSE, *n.f.s.* youth; 82:6; 86:16

LABOUR, *n.f.s.* pain, torment; 42:24; 62:19: LABEUR work, labour; 46:8; 46:12

LACHEMENT, *adv.* basely, shamefully; 76:27

LAIDURE, *n.f.s.* ugliness, wickedness, unpleasantness; 25:3; 49:18

LAIZ, (i) *1st s.pr.ind.* of *tr.v.* LAISSIER to leave; 70:6 (ii) *n.m.pl.* lays; 46:5

LAME, *n.f.s.* blade; 75:12

LANGOUR, *n.f.s.* langour; 62:3

LANGUIR, *infin.* of *intr.v.* to languish; 26:7: LANGUI *1st s.pr.ind.*; 15:33; 25:40: LANGUIST *3rd s.pr.ind.*; 88:3

LAREZ, *imp. 2nd pl.* of *tr.v.* LAÏER to leave; 34:19

LARGAICHE, see LARGESSE

LARGEMENT, *adv.* liberally; 90:23

LARGES, *a.m.s.* liberal; 5:23

LARGESSE/LARGAICHE, *n.f.s.* liberality; 28:16; 86:5: À LARGESSE in quantity; 88:10

LARMOIER, *infin.* of *intr.v.* to weep; 12:22: LARMOYE *1st s.pr.ind.*; 68:11

LAS, (i) *a.m.s.* weary; 53:9; 62:11; 87:3 (ii) *int.* alas!; 59:45; 75:15

LASCHE, *n.m.s.* coward; 88:15

LASSER, *infin.* of *refl.v.* to grow weary; 87:15

LAURIQUE, *n.f.s.* knight's hauberc; 55:31

LAY, *imp. 2nd s.* of *tr.v.* LAÏER to leave; 11:15

LAZ, *n.m.pl.* nets, traps; 43:34

LERMES, *n.f.pl.* tears; 77:12; 88:10

LESIR, *n.f.s.* leisure: A LESIR at leisure; 2:14

LEVERENT, *3rd pl.past def.* of *tr.v.* LEVER to raise (to the baptismal fount); 48:17

LIE/LYÉE, *a.f.s.* happy, joyful; 40:32; 56:15; 89:38: LIEZ *a.m.s.*; 6:7

LIEMENT, *adv.* gladly; 46:15; 65:17; 84:10

LIÉS, *2nd pl.pr.ind.* of *tr.v.* LIER to bind, grip; 2:18

LÏESSE, *n.f.s.* happiness; 86:2; 93:3; 99:5

LIEULX, *n.m.pl.* places; 96:4

LIEVÉ, *past part.* of *tr.v.* LIEVER to raise; 28:12

LINAGE, *n.m.s.* family, birth; 29:8

LIST/LIT, *3rd s.pr.ind.* of *tr.v.* LIRE to read; 87:3; 87:12

LIVRÉE, *n.f.s.* livery; 97:9; 100:6

LO, see LOËR

LOËR/LOUËR, *infin.* of *tr.v.* to praise; 33:5; 40:1; 87:13: LOE/LO *1st s.pr. ind.*; 58:13; 69:2; 69:11: LOE *3rd s.pr.ind.*; 21:5: LOËNT *3rd pl.pr.ind.*; 40:16: LOUEZ *past part.*; 61:5

LOGIS, *n.m.s.* dwelling; 88:2

LOIER, *n.m.s.* reward; 43:13

LOINGS, *a.m.s.* far-off; 86:19; 89:7

LONGTAIN, *a.m.s.* distant; 75:9

LONS, *a.m.pl.* long; 60:11

LOUR, *poss.a.* their; 76:30

LUY, *1st s.past def.* of LIRE to read; 57:5

LUYANT, *a.m.s.* shining; 97:4

LYÉE, see LIE

MAIN, *n.m.s.* morning; 44:34; 56:23;
91:15; 100:4

MAINS: AU MAINS at least; 92:18

MAINT/MAYNT, (i) *3rd s.pr.ind.* of *intr.v.*
MANOIR to stay, dwell; 2:2; 9:2;
16:14: MAINT (ii) *a.m.s.* many (a);
2:4; 16:7; 25:10; 46:21; 48:15;
59:25; 59:44; 88:8; 90:15: many a
man; 9:5; 53:14; 53:22: MAINTE
a.f.s.; 55:9; 55:21; 60:24; 89:5; 92:8;
MAINTES *a.f.pl.*; 52:5; 100:7

MAINTIEN, *n.m.s.* manner, way (of
conduct); 61:22; 62:13: EN SI FAIT
MAINTIEN in this way; 61:22

MAIS, *adv.* more; 68:1

MAISTROIE, *3rd s.pr.ind.* of *tr.v.*
MAISTROÏER to master; 19:20; 75:14

MALE, *a.f.s.* painful; 64:5

MALEÜRÉE, *a.f.s.* wretched, unhappy;
62:3

MALLEMENT, *adv.* badly, wickedly; 90:3

MANIER, *infin.* of *tr.v.* to deal with; 29:16

MANT, *1st s.pr.ind.* of *tr.v.* MANDER to
send; 5:3

MANTIAUX, *n.m.pl.* coats; 60:22

MAPEMONDE, *n.f.s.* map of the world;
36:2

MARGHERITE, *n.f.s.* daisy; 37:9

MARRAINE, *n.f.s.* godmother; 48:26

MARTIR, *n.m.s.* martyr; 88:24

MARTIRE, (i) *n.m.s.* agony; 45:24;
70:11 (ii) *3rd s.pr.ind.* of *tr.v.* MAR-
TIRER to torment, massacre; 66:3

MASURE, *n.f.s.* dwelling; 31:11

MAUGRÉ, *prep.* in spite of; 13:23; 95:9

MAULS/MAULX/MAULZ/MAUS,
n.m.pl. evils, discomforts; 1:7; 6:25;
26:5; 43:5; 54:7; 86:15

MAUPARLIERE, *a.f.s.* slanderous; 1:10

MAYNT, see MAINT (i)

MEFFEROIE, *1st s.cond.* of *intr.v.*
MEFFERE to do wrong; 20:8

MEINENT, *3rd pl.pr.ind.* of *tr.v.* MENER
to carry on; 74:19

MEMBRE, *1st s.pr.ind.* of *refl.v.* MEMBRER
to remember; 48:10

MENDRES D'ANS, LES, the two infants
(minors); 56:28

MENEUR, *sup.a.m.s.* least; 10:10

MERCY, *n.f.s.*: LA SIENNE MERCY
thanks to her; 86:6

MERI, *n.m.s.* merit; 25:41

MESAISIÉE, *past part.f.* of *tr.& intr.v.*
MESAISIER to suffer; 63:5

MESCHIEF, *n.m.s.* misfortune; 2:4;
67:10: MESCHIÉS/MESCHIEZ
n.m.pl.; 12:20; 55:28

MESDIRE, *infin.* of *intr.v.* to slander,
speak ill; 20:26; 45:4

MESDISANS, *n.m.pl.* slanderers,
gossips; 85:1

MESMES, *a.m.s.* self; 87:15

MESPRENDRE, *infin.* of *intr.v.* to do
wrong; 69:12

MESPRISE, *3rd s.pr.ind.* of *tr.v.* MES-
PRISER to scorn; 69:15

MESSE, *n.f.s.* mass; 88:21

MESTIER, (i) *n.m.s.* need; 69:18 (ii)
n.m.pl. officers; 55:23

METZ, *1st s.pr.ind.* of *tr.v.* METRE to put;
91:18

MI:EN MI in the middle, in half; 25:19

MIE, *a.f.s.* mid; 48:24

MIEUDRE, *comp. a.f.s.* better; 10:6:
a.m.s.; 44:6

MIEX/MIEULZ, *adv.* better; 5:36; 15:21;
20:6 etc.

MINE, *3rd s.pr.ind.* of *tr.v.* MINER to
undermine, exhaust; 58:15: MINÉ
past part.; 24:56

MINIERES, *n.f.pl.* mines; 53:26

MIRE, (i) *n.m.s.* doctor; 66:15 (ii) *3rd
s.pr.subj.* of *tr.v.* MIRER to heal, cure;
70:3

MIRON, *imp. 1st pl.* of *tr.v.* MIRER to admire; 59:33

MONDAINS, *a.m.s.* earthly; 51:3; 59:51: MONDAINE *a.f.s.*; 54:13

MONDE, *a.f.s.* pure; 17:12; 27:15; 36:5; 67:3

MONJOIE, *n.f.s.* summit of delight; 78:9

MONNOYE, *n.f.s.* money; 82:6

MONTEPLIE, *3rd s.pr.ind.* of *intr.v.* MONTEPLIER to increase; 57:9

MORDRIST, see MURDRIT

MORÉE, *n.f.s.* dark brown; 63:24

MORIR/MOURIR, *infin.* of *intr.v.* to die; 20:6; 34:21; 72:13; 93:5: MUIR/MUERS *1st s.pr.ind.*; 19:30; 92:1: MUERT *3rd s.pr.ind.*; 49:26: MUIRE *1st s.pr.subj.*; 1:2: MORRAY *1st s.fut.*; 15:34; 72:6: MOURRÉS *2nd pl.fut.*; 89:13: MOURRONT *3rd pl.fut.*; 59:10: MORROIE/MOURROYE *1st s.cond.*; 20:17; 75:7: MOURUT *3rd s.past def.*; 55:10: MORT *past part.* of *tr.v.* MORIR to kill; 24:56

MORS, *a.m.s.* dead; 34:7

MORTELZ/MORTIEULX, *a.m.s.* mortal; 59:45; 74:33: MORTELLE *a.f.s.*; 89:44

MOS, *n.m.s.* word; 7:14

MOULT, *adv.* very; 42:1; 45:2; 55:11; 55:14; 60:31; 88:23; 89:21

MOVER, *infin.* of *tr.v.* to move, change; 30:20

MOYE, *poss.a.f.* my; 68:12

MOYS, *n.m.pl.* months; 50:20

MUCIÉE, *past part.f.* of *tr.v.* MUCIER to hide; 63:9

MUËR, *infin.* of *tr.v.* to change, transform; 17:20: MUEZ *past part.m.pl.*; 52:12

MUERT, see MORIR

MUGET, *n.m.s.* Lily of the valley; 37:6

MURDRIT/MURTRIT/MORDRIST, *3rd s.pr.ind.* of *tr.v.* MURDRIR to kill, murder; 12:21; 26:10; 76:11

MY, *emphatic pers. pron. 1st s.* (moi) me; 52:13

NAFFRE, see NAVRE

NATURÏEN, *n.m.s.* scholar, naturalist; 59:5

NAVIRON, *n.m.s.* ship, vessel; 36:10

NAVRE/NAFFRE, *3rd s.pr.ind.* of *tr.v.* NAVRER to stab, wound; 79:12: NAVRÉ/NAVRÉS *past part.*; 24:16; 34:5; 37:22

NEANTMOINS, *adv.* nevertheless; 77:15

NEGE, *n.f.s.* snow; 100:10

NEL, *contraction* of NE LE; 75:25

NENNIL, *adv.* no, not at all; 99:14

NEPOURQUANT, *adv.* nevertheless; 7:21; 30:5

NESUNE, *indefinite a.f.s.* none at all; 76:4

NETTE, *a.f.s.* pure, perfect; 34:9; 37:11

NEZ, *past part.* of *intr.v.* NAISTRE to be born; 76:1

NÏENT, *adv.* none: NÏENT MAINS none the less; 27:18

NO *poss. adj. 1st pl.* our; 31:5; 31:11; 54:22

NOM/NON *n.m.s.* renown; 28:4; 59:13: NON name; 28:19

NOMPAREILLE, *a.f.s.* peerless, without equal; 57:2; 89:8

NON, see NOM

NONCHALOIR, *n.m.s.* lassitude, resignation; 20:47; 91:1

NONPOURQUANT, *adv.* nevertheless; 20:10; 24:53

NÖOIT, *3rd s.imperf.* of *intr.v.* NOÏER to drown; 36:11: NOYE *3rd s.pr.ind.*; 40:15

NOTOIRE, *a.f.s.* manifest; 55:13

NOURRY, *past part.* of *tr.v.* NOURRIR to nourish; 89:34

NOUVELLETÉ, *n.f.s.* fickleness, desire for change; 14:6

NOYE, see NÖOIT

NUISANCE, *n.f.s.* injury, harm; 77:7

NUIT, *3rd s.pr.ind.* of *tr.v.* NUIRE to harm; 58:33

NULLI/NULLUY, *pron.* no⁄one; 30:12; 98:9

NULZ/NUS, *indefinite a.m.s.* no, not one, no⁄one; 28:17; 59:27

O, *prep.* with; 55:34

OBSCUREMENT, *adv.* dimly; 62:5

OBSEQUE, *n.f.s.* obsequy, obsequies; 52:9

OCIÉS, *2nd pl.pr.ind.* of *tr.v.* OCIRE to kill; 24:6: OCCIT *3rd s.past def.*; 12:2; 76:28: OCY *past part.*; 35:7

OCTROYE, *1st s.pr.ind.* of *refll.v.* OCTROYER to abandon onself, surrender; 95:3

OFRANDE, *n.f.s.* offering; 55:23

OÏR/OUÏR, *infin.* of *tr.v.* to hear, listen to; 20:14; 38:14; 45:6: OY *1st s.pr.ind.*; 58:2; 65:2; 88:9: OYT *3rd s.pr.ind.*; 87:12: OIE/OYE *3rd s.pr.subj.*; 20:46; 95:6: OÏ *1st s.past def.*; 42:7: OY *imp. 2nd s.*; 16:1: OŸ *past part.*; 43:1

OISEUX, *a.m.pl.* lazy; 44:21

ONQUES/ONCQUES, *adv.* never; 12:5; 20:1; 24:55 etc.

ORDENANCE/ORDONNANCE, *n.f.s.* judgement, decision, ruling; 77:19; 100:8

ORDENÉEMENT *adv.* in order; 38:17

ORDONNANCE, see ORDENANCE

ORE, *adv.* now; 5:35; 37:19

ORENT, see HA

ORFAVERIE, *n.f.s.* jewellery; 97:10

ORGUE, *n.f.s.* organum, harmony; 50:5

ORT, *a.m.s.* filthy; 64:6

OSTÉ/OSTEZ, *past part.* of *tr.v.* OSTER to remove; 31:10; 46:23: OSTÉS/OSTEZ *imp. 2nd pl.*; 67:5; 70:19

OT, see HA

OTTRI, (i) *1st s.pr.ind.* of *tr.v.* OTRÏER to give, grant; 25:2 (ii) see OTROI

OTROI/OTTRI, *n.m.s.* gift, authorisation; 6:15; 23:42

OUIL, *adv.* yes; 86:10

OULTRAGE, *n.m.s.* sin, outrage; 59:48; 61:11

OULTRE, *prep.* beyond; 58:35

OUTRAGIEUX, *a.m.pl.* outrageous; 89:41

OUVRER, *infin.* of *intr.v.* to work; 20:41: OVRE *3rd s.pr.subj.*; 31:12

OY, OŸ, OYT, see OÏR

OYSIAULX, *n.m.pl.* birds; 74:14

PACIENS, *a.m.s.* suffering; 49:23

PAIEN, *a.m.s.* pagan; 59:12

PAILLE, *n.f.s.* straw; 99:11

PAÏS, *n.m.s.* country; 55:16; 75:9

PANON, see PENON

PARACHEVEZ, *imp. 2nd pl.* of *tr.v.* PARACHEVER to finish off; 81:12

PARAGE, *n.m.s.* rank, high birth; 29:15; 59:53

PARÇONNIERS, *n.m.pl.* sharers, partners; 94:4

PARÉE, *past part.f.* of *tr.v.* PARER to attire, adorn; 84:9

PAREILLEMENT, *adv.* similarly; 98:2

PAREULX, *a.m.pl.* similar: 44:14

PARFAICTE, *past part.f.* of *tr.v.* PARFAIRE to complete; 55:21

PARFONT, *a.m.s.* deep; 62:10: PARFONDE *a.f.s.*; 18:2; 27:23; 36:11; 67:8

PARFOURNIR, *infin.* of *tr.v.* to achieve one's ends; 45:16

PARRAINS, *n.m.s.* godfather; 48:28

PARS, *n.m.pl.* parks; 13:22

PART, *n.f.s.* prize; 78:9

PARTUE, *3rd s.pr.ind.* of *tr.v.* PARTUER to kill, finish off; 12:23

PARTY, *n.m.s.* state; 86:17

PAS, *n.m.pl.* narrow passages, straits; 53:6

PASCHOUR, *a.m.s.* easter, spring; 74:20

PASME, *3rd s.pr.ind.* of *intr.v.* PASMER to swoon; 75:29

PASSEROSE, *n.f.s.* Hollyhock, Rose-mallow; 32:1

PECCUNE, *n.f.s.* money, riches; 76:29

PEL, *n.f.s.* skin; 27:21; 64:18

PENON/PANON, *n.m.s.* pennant; 28:12; 59:43

PENRE, *infin.* of *tr.v.* (form of PRENDRE) to wage; 18:19

PENSEMENT, *n.m.s.* project, plan; 90:9

PER, *n.f.s.* equal, peer; 26:9; 87:10

PERDRIX, *n.f.pl.* partridges; 56:20

PERESSE, *n.f.s.* indolence; 88:19

PERS, *1st s.pr.ind.* of *tr.v.* PERDRE to lose; 58:3; 92:8

PERSELLE, *n.f.s.* Cornflower; 37:3

PERTE, *n.f.s.* loss; 68:3

PESANCE, *n.f.s.* distress; 2:17; 66:23

PETIT, *adv.* little; 37:25; 45:2

PIEÇA, *adv.* some time ago; 76:8; 86:38; 91:2

PILLARS, *n.m.s.* thief, plunderer; 13:14

PIS:JE LES METZ AU PIS I let them do their worst; 91:18

PLAIN, (i) *adv.* plainly; 100:12 (ii) *a.m.s.* full; 86:2; 100:9: PLAINS (i) *a.m.pl.*; 33:1 (ii) *1st s.pr.ind.* of *tr.v.* PLAINDRE to lament, bemoan; 68:1; 68:8; 98:11: PLAINT *3rd s.pr.ind.*; 88:26: PLAINGNENT *3rd pl.pr.ind.*; 90:4 (iii) *n.m.pl.* lamentations; 76:15 (iv) *n.m.pl.* plains; 53:19

PLAISE, *3rd s.pr.subj.* of *tr.v.* PLAIRE to please; 66:15: PLEÜ *past part.*; 50:11

PLENIERE, *a.f.s.* complete; 40:30

PLEÜ, see PLAISE

PLEVIS, *1st s.pr.ind.* of *tr.v.* PLEVIR to promise, pledge; 60:38

PLOURS, *n.m.pl.* weeping, lamentation; 52:9

PLUEVE, *3rd s.pr.subj.* of *intr.v.* PLEUVOIR to rain; 37:10

PLUYE, *n.f.s.* rain; 97:2, 100:10

PO/POU/POY, *adv.* little, hardly; 44:14; 47:19; 64:18; 98:4

POINGNANT, *a.f.s.* piercing, poignant; 24:33

POINS, *n.m.pl.* points, topics; 38:7

POINT, (i) *3rd s.pr.ind.* of *tr.v.* POINDRE to stab, wound; 43:36 (ii) :EN BON POINT extremely fit; 91:5

POINTURE, *n.f.s.* stabbing; 19:17; 34:6; 66:2

POISSANT, *a.m.s.* powerful; 59:23

POLLETIQUE, *a.m.s.* prudent, wise; 59:46

PÖOIR, *n.m.s.* power; 28:9; 41:7

POROYE, see POVOYE

POU, *n.m.s.* few; 59:41

POUR, *prep.* because of, through; 81:5

POURCEVOIR, *infin.* of *tr.v.* to establish, bring about; 44:19

POURQUISE, *n.f.s.* search, endeavour; 69:21

POURSUÏS, *past part.* of *tr.v.* POURSUÏR to pursue; 53:12

POURTRAIS, *past part.* of *tr.v.* POURTRAIRE to portray; 10:12

POVOYE, *1st s.imperf.* of *intr.v.* POVOIR/POOIR to be able; 82:5: POROYE *1st s.condit.*; 83:16: POZ *1st s.past def.*; 71:16

POVRE, *a.m.s.* impoverished; 92:4

POY, see PO

POZ, see POVOYE

PRACTICÏEN, *n.m.s.* doctor; 59:2

PRACTIQUE, *n.f.s.* practice, achievement; 50:22

PRAMIS, *past part.* of *tr.v.* PRAMETRE to promise; 7:29

PREMIEREMENT *adv.* in the first instance; 77:5

PRENG/PREING/PRENS, *1st s.pr.ind.* of *tr.v.* PRENDRE to take; 8:6; 9:8; 18:11; 89:12: PREINGE/PRAINGNE *3rd s.pr.subj.*; 31:17; 54:18

PREST, (i) *n.m.s.* loan; 46:4 (ii) *a.m.s.* ready, prepared; 45:8: PRESTE *a.f.s.*; 59:49

PRESTEZ, *past part.m.pl.* of *tr.v.* PRESTER to lend; 46:1: PRESTRAY *1st s.fut.*; 46:10

PREU/PROU, *n.m.s.* profit, advantage; 22:8; 81:7

PREUX, *a.m.s.* valiant; 44:9

PRIMIER, *adv.* first of all; 82:13

PRIS, *n.m.s.* worth, value; 11:14; 18:3; 21:6; 29:6; 53:35

PRISIER, *infin.* of *tr.v.* to esteem, value; 14:3; 39:23: PRISE *1st s.pr.ind.*; 69:1: PRISE *3rd s.pr.ind.*; 21:5

PRIVEZ, *a.m.pl.* intimate; 94:10

PROCHAINEMENT, *adv.* soon; 27:4

PRODOM/PRODOMME, *n.m.s.* loyal man, valiant man; 48:28; 55:19

PROFFIS, *n.m.pl.* borders, edges to dresses; 60:23

PROFIT, *3rd s.pr.ind.* of *tr.v.* PROFITER to benefit; 30:21

PROMETTRE, *infin.* of *tr.v.* to promise; 79:2

PROPREMENT, *adv.* properly speaking; 77:2: neatly, beautifully; 84:10

PROU, see PREU

PROUESSE, *n.f.s.* valour; 28:3: PROUESCES *n.f.pl.*; 55:4

PROUFFIT, *n.m.s.* benefit; 92:23

PROYE, *3rd s.pr.ind.* of *tr.v.* PROIER to pray, beg; 75:30

PRUNE, *n.f.s.*: JE NE COMPTE UNE PRUNE I do not have a penny; 76:16

PSALTERÏON, *n.m.s.* psaltery; 51:18

PUCELLE, *n.f.s.* maiden; 33:3

PUGNICÏON, *n.f.s.* punishment; 54:22

PUIS, (i) *adv.* since; 5:12; 48:4; 55:33; 71:16 (ii) *n.m.s.* well; 11:17

PUNAISIE, *n.f.s.* infection; 56:7

PUNIQUE, *a.f.s.* savage, intense; 55:7; 59:16

PYONE, *n.f.s.* Peony; 37:6

QUANQUE/QUANQU'/QUANQUI, *neuter pron.* whatever, everything that; 41:3; 65:8; 76:18; 98:5

QUARTE, *a.f.s.* (QUITTE?) blameless, free from guilt; 27:15

QUERELLE, *n.f.s.* aim, object; 60:44

QUERIR, *infin.* of *tr.v.* to seek; 31:2; 31:5; 45:7: QUERANT *pr.part.*; 99:3

QUIER, *1st s.pr.ind.* of *tr.v.* QUERRE to seek; 11:8; 12:8; 17:1; 32:5; 36:1: QUIERE *3rd s.pr.subj.*; 67:9; 67:10: QUISE *past part.f.*; 69:19

QUIEUX, *interr.pron.* who?; 73:3

QUOIE, see COIE

RADE, *a.f.s.* rough, tempestuous; 36:11

RAINS, *n.f.pl.* hips; 60:14

RAINSEAU, *n.m.s.* branch; 77:26

RAMENTEVOIR, *infin.* of *tr.v.* to recall to mind; 44:27; 46:6

RANCUNE, *n.f.s.* spite, malice; 76:26

RANSONNOIE, *3rd s.imperf.* of *tr.v.* RANSONNER to ransom; 79:11

RAPAISER, *infin.* of *tr.v.* to calm down; 87:23

RAVOYE, *3rd s.pr.subj.* of *tr.v.* RAVOIER to set back on the right path; 67:6

REBEBE, *n.f.s.* rebec; 51:17

REBOURS, :À REBOURS backwards, against the grain; 90:17

RECHIGNER, *infin.* of *intr.v.* to grimace; 64:11: RECHIGNEZ *past part.pl.* grimacing; 65:4

RECLAIMS, *n.m.pl.* prayers, cries; 68:31

RECLAME, *1st s.pr.ind.* of *tr.v.* RE⁄
CLAMER to call for, implore; 75:28

RECLUS, *past part.* of *tr.v.* RECLORE to
shut up, enclose; 86:32

RECORS, *a.m.s.* mindful; 57:15

RECOURS, (i) *n.m.pl.* recourse, salvation;
52:16 (ii) *a.m.s.* (from *tr.v.* RESCORRE)
recaptured; 95:4

RECOUVRER, *infin.* of *tr.v.* to recover,
regain; 86:19

RECRÉEZ, *imp. 2nd pl.* of *tr.v.* RE⁄
CRÉER to revive; 52:20

RECROIE, *1st s.pr.subj.* of *intr.v.* RE⁄
CROIRE to renounce, give up; 20:35

RECUIT, *a.m.pl.* reluctant, recalcitrant;
54:11

REÇUY, *1st s.past def.* of *tr.v.* RECEVOIR
to receive; 57:25

REDIGEZ, *past part.m.pl.* of *tr.v.*
REDIGER to reduce; 59:19

REDIRE: NE TREUVE À REDIRE can
find no fault with; 65:20

REDONDE, *3rd s.pr.ind.* of *intr.v.*
REDONDER to be abundant; 18:12

REDOUBTE, *1st s.pr.ind.* of *tr.v.*
REDOUBTER to fear; 96:3

REDRESSE, *3rd s.pr.subj.* of *tr.v.*
REDRESSER to rectify, put right;
99:14

REFAIS, *past part.* of *tr.v.* REFAIRE to
restore, heal; 7:21; 7:22; 10:4

REGREZ, *n.m.pl.* regrets, lamentations;
76:15

REMAINDRE, *infin.* of *intr.v.* to remain;
71:4: REMAINT *3rd s.pr.ind.*; 88:15

REMIRER, *infin.* of *tr.v.* to regard; 19:5;
20:13: REMIR *1st s.pr.ind.*; 5:10

REMORT, *3rd s.pr.ind.* of *tr.v.* RE⁄
MORDRE to give remorse; 58:18

REMUER, *infin.* of *intr.v.* to change; 19:40

RENTIERE, *n.f.s.* owner, possessor; 67:13

REPAIRE, (i) *3rd s.pr.ind.* of *intr.v.*
REPAIRIER to dwell; 22:1 (ii)
n.m.s. dwelling; 22:3

REPAISTRE, *infin.* of *refl.v.* to feed one's
self, take one's fill of; 63:10

REPAST, *n.m.s.* meal; 99:10

REPLIQUE, *n.f.s.* rejoinder, argument;
59:27

REPRANDRE, *infin.* of *tr.v.* to blame,
criticise; 46:25: REPRISE *past part.f.*;
69:10

REQUERIR, *infin.* of *tr.v.* to seek; 46:18;
86:23

REQUERRE, *infin.* of *tr.v.* to seek,
request; 15:19: REQUIER *1st s.pr.ind.*;
76:31; 88:20; 93:4: REQUIERT *3rd
s.pr.ind.*; 40:25; 50:18: REQUISE
past part.f. (wooed); 69:18

REQUOY, *n.m.s.* secret; 34:14

RESJOYE, *3rd s.pr.subj.* of *tr.v.*
RESJOÏR to gladden; 83:12

RESPASSE, *3rd s.pr.ind.* of *intr.v.*
RESPASSER to get better, be cured;
49:24

RESPIT, *n.m.s.* respite; 87:17

RESPITE, *3rd s.pr.ind.* of *tr.v.* RE⁄
SPITER to respite, spare; 37:25

RESTRAINGNE, *3rd s.pr.subj.* of *tr.v.*
RESTRAINDRE to restrain, protect;
54:20

RESVER, *infin.* of *intr.v.* to dream; 61:21

RETHOURYQUE, *n.m.s.* poet, man of
letters; 50:8

RETING, *1st s.past def.* of *tr.v.* RETENIR
to retain; 6:10

RETOUR, *n.m.s.* reward, cure; 42:27;
70:26: RETOURS *n.m.pl.*; 6:11

RETRAIRE, *infin.* of *tr.v.* to withdraw;
8:3; 22:6: RETRAIS *past part.m.*;
7:15; 7:14 (to say, express):
RETRAITE *past part.f.*; 7:16 (to
express)

RETRANCHAST, see RETRENCHIER

RETRENCHIER, *infin.* of *tr.v.* to cut back, prune; 77:33: RETRANCHAST *3rd s.imperf.subj.*; 77:25

REUME, *n.m.s.* cold; 49:17

REÜSER, *infin.* of *intr.v.* to deceive; 7:27

REVEL, *a.m.s.* rebellious; 27:22

REVELLEUX, *a.m.s.* revealing; 44:17

REVEST, *3rd s.pr.ind.* of *tr.v.* REVESTIR to clothe; 100:5

RIBAUS, *n.m.s.* rogue; 13:14

RIEULE, *n.f.s.* rule, system; 38:18

RIS, *n.m.s.* laughter; 78:3

ROINE/ROYONE,*n.f.s.* queen; 31:10; 48:7

ROMMANT, *n.m.s.* romance; 87:4

RONT, *a.m.s.* round; 60:8: RONDES *a.m.pl.*; 60:18

ROSTIE, *past part.f.* of *tr.v.* ROSTIR to roast; 56:19

ROUSSIGNOL, *n.m.s.* nightingale; 35:1

ROUTE, *n.f.s.* troop, band; 13:23; 96:10

ROUVER, *infin.* of *tr.v.* to request, ask for; 15:12; 61:15: ROUVÉ *past part.*; 24:40

ROUVERTE, *past part.f.* of *tr.v.* ROUVRIR to re⁄open; 68:28

ROYONE, see ROINE

RUISSEL, *n.m.s.* stream; 51:10

RUSÉ, :JE FEROYE FORT DU RUSÉ I would act with great cunning; 82:14

SA, : OR SA *int.* now then!; 95:11

SABMEDI, *n.m.s.* Saturday; 48:20

SACRE, *n.m.s.* coronation, consecration; 55:33

SAFRAIN, *n.m.s.* saffron; 56:21

SAICHANS, *n.m.pl.* wise men; 92:4

SAICHENT, see SARA

SAIGE/SAIGES, *a.m.s.* wise; 53:32; 55:3; 59:10

SAIN, *n.m.s.* breast; 60:10

SAINS, (i) *a.m.s.* well, in good health; 68:19

SAINT, *n.m.s.* saint; 88:24: SAINS, (ii) *n.m.pl.*; 13:3

SAJETTE, *n.f.s.* arrow; 37:22

SALUS, *n.f.pl.* greetings; 5:3

SAMBLANCE, *n.f.s.* appearance; 25:36

SAMBLANT, *n.m.s.* appearance; 24:10

SANTINE, *n.f.s.* bilge water; 58:22

SANZ, *prep.* without; 62:3; 62:13, etc.

SAOULER, *infin.* of *tr.v.* to intoxicate, make drunk; 20:23

SARA/SÇARA, *3rd s.fut.* of *tr.v.* SAVOIR to know; 14:22; 48:9: SARAS/SÇARAS *2nd s.fut.*; 28:19; 57:27: SAROIT *3rd s.condit.*; 14:1: SCET *3rd s.pr.ind.*; 48:14; 53:10; 86:17; 87:27: SCEVENT *3rd pl.pr.ind.*; 85:3: SAICHENT *3rd pl.pr.subj.*; 48:20

SARACYNOIS, *a.m.pl.* Saracen; 51:15

SÇARA, see SARA

SCET, see SARA

SCEVENT, see SARA

SECHIER, *infin.* of *intr.v.* to dry up; 77:8

SECONDE, *a.f.s.* rival; 17:10; 36:18; 67:14

SECOUX, *imp. 2nd s.* of *tr.v.* SECOURRE to shake; 64:17

SEGNOUR, *n.m.s.* lord; 55:11: SEIGNEURS *n.m.pl.*; 50:12

SEMONDRE, *infin.* of *tr.v.* to summon; 43:19

SENTEMENT, *n.m.s.* feeling, mood; 38:9

SENZ, *1st s.pr.ind.* of *tr.v.* SENTIR to feel; 5:9

SËOIR, *infin.* of *intr.v.* to sit; 37:21: SIET *3rd s.pr.ind.*; 27:6: SIÉE *3rd s.pr.subj.*; 63:16: SIÉE *3rd s.pr.subj.* of impersonal *v.* SËOIR to suit, please; 63:12

SEPMAINE, *n.f.s.* week; 92:8

SEUFFRE/SUEFRE, *1st s.pr.ind.* of *tr.v.*
SOUFRIR to suffer; 4:3; 34:17

SEULZ, *a.m.s.* alone, separate; 44:2

SEUR, (i) *prep.* over, above; 17:23 (ii)
a.m.s. sure, certain; 89:28: SEÜRE
a.f.s.; 24:43; 31:5; 31:16

SI, *poss. pron. (pl. of 3rd s.* SON) his; 13:7

SIÉE, see SËOIR

SIET, see SËOIR

SIRES, *n.m.s.* lord; 46:29

SIXTE, *a.m.s.* sixth; 48:13

SOFFISTES, *n.m.pl.* sophists; 50:3

SOIGN, *imp. 1st pl.* of *v.* ESTRE to be;
54:9

SOLAS, see SOULAS

SOLOYE, *1st s.imperf.* of *intr.v.* SOLOIR
to be accustomed; 82:1; 83:5

SON, *n.m.s.* sound; 36:3

SONGNEUX, *a.m.s.* careful; 92:5

SOUBZ, *prep.* beneath; 74:27; 75:12;
76:20

SOUFFIRE, *infin.* of *intr.v.* to suffice;
70:17: SOUFFIST *3rd. s.pr.ind.*; 46:11

SOUFFISANCE, *n.f.s.* efficiency,
mastery; 57:18

SOUFFRANCE, *n.f.s.*: EN SOUFFRANCE
waste, uncultivated; 77:17

SOUFFREZ, *imp. 2nd pl.* of *tr.v.*
SOUFFRIR to permit; 77:34; 81:15

SOUFRE, *n.m.s.* sulphur; 53:24

SOUHAIDIER, *infin.* of *tr.v.* to wish; 29:19:
SOUHAIDENT *3rd pl.pr.ind.*; 58:35

SOULAS/SOLAS, *n.m.s.* solace, pleasure;
40:25; 67:6; 82:2

SOUPE'ÇON, *n.f.s.* suspicion; 89:32

SOURCIS, *n.m.pl.* eyebrows; 60:6

SOURS, *a.m.s.* muffled, muted; 52:11

SOUSPRAINGNE, *3rd s.pr.subj.* of *tr.v.*
SOUSPRENDRE to take by surprise;
54:23

SOUSSI/SOUSSY, *n.m.s.* care, anxiety;
62:17; 86:18

SOUSSIE, *n.f.s.* Marigold; 37:6

SOUSSY, see SOUSSI

SOUSTENANCE, *n.f.s.* sustenance;
77:16

SOUTIEX, see SUTILS

SOUVENANCE, *n.f.s.* memory; 48:30;
77:34

SOUVERAIN, *a.m.s.* extreme; 87:14

SUEFRE, see SEUFFRE

SUER, *n.f.s.* sister; 57:31

SUPPOSÉ: PAR SUPPOSÉ in expecta-
tion (?); 82:8

SURMONTER, *infin.* of *tr.v.* to overcome;
87:20

SUS, *prep.* on; 62:6; 91:2

SUTILS/SOUTIEUX, *a.m.s.* subtle; 5:34;
53:31

TABIS, *n.m.s.* watered silk; 60:26

TAILLE, *3rd s.pr.ind.* of *tr.v.* TAILLER
to tax; 43:38

TAINT, *3rd s.pr.ind.* of *tr.v.* TAINDRE to
colour; 16:16; 26:10: TAINT *past
part.m.*; 2:20: TAINTE *past part.f.*;
63:24

TALENT/TALANT, *n.m.s.* will, wish,
desire, inclination; 1:6; 89:33

TANCE, see TENCIER

TANT: TANT NE QUANT in no way;
99:4

TARIR, *infin.* of *intr.v.* to run dry; 62:14

TART, *adv.* late; 42:1

TELEMENT, *adv.* in such a way; 84:11

TELX, *a.m.s.* such; 82:1: TIEULX/
TIEUX *a.m.pl.*; 5:33; 74:10; 74:28

TEMPREMENT, *adv.* soon; 15:34

TEMS, *n.m.s.* time: DES LONG TEMS A
for a long time; 77:11

TENCIER, *infin.* of *tr.v.* to scold; 64:11:
TENSE *1st s.pr.ind.*; 91:15: TANCE/
TENSE *3rd s.pr.ind.*; 65:10; 87:19

TENÇON, *n.f.s.* battle, quarrel; 18:19

TENDRAY, *1st s.fut.* of *tr.v.* TENIR to hold, keep, adhere to; 86:32: TENROIE/TENDROYE *1st s.condit.*; 40:17; 95:10

TENROUR, *n.f.s* tenderness; 25:12

TENSE, see TENCIER

TERESTRIN, *a.m.s.* earthy; 27:2

TERMES, *n.m.s.* term, day of return; 46:3

TERRIEN, *a.m.s.* earthly; 59:44

TESMOING, *n.m.s.* witness; 100:3

TI *poss. pron.* (*pl.* of *2nd s.* TON) your; 11:23

TIERS, *a.m.s.* third; 48:1

TIEULX/TIEUX, see TELX

TIMPANE, *n.f.s.* tambourine; 51:21

TOISON, *n.f.s.* fleece; 18:17

TON: SOIT À BAS OU HAULT TON (whether at high pitch or low) inevitably, whatever the circumstances; 59:55

TONDRE, *infin.* of *tr.v.* to cut; 43:33: TONDE *3rd s.pr.subj.*; 17:4 (cut hair)

TOST, *adv.* soon, swiftly; 20:43; 36:16; 75:6; 86:35

TOUDIS/TOUSDIS/TOUT DIS, *adv.* always; 5:8; 25:18; 42:32; 45:14; 58:28

TOULU, *past part.* of *tr.v.* TOLDRE to remove, carry off; 76:22

TOUX, *n.f.s.* cough; 49:17: *n.f.pl.*; 64:10

TRAIS, (i) *past part.m.* of *refl.v.* TRAIRE to come to, affect; 7:24: TRAITE *past part.f.* of *tr.v.* TRAIRE to obtain, draw out; 7:26
(ii) *n.m.pl.* traits, features; 7:5; 10:10

TRAÏSON, *n.m.s.* treachery; 89:2

TRAITIS, *a.m.s.* pretty; 60:7

TRAMIS, *past part.* of *tr.v.* TRAMETRE to send, transmit; 7:19; 53:24

TRAVAIL/TRAVEIL, *n.m.s.* trial, torment; 53:8; 62:20: TRAVAULX *n.m.pl.*; 43:2

TRAVAILLE, *3rd s.pr.ind.* of *tr.v.* TRAVAILLER to torture; 43:36

TRAVAULX, see TRAVAIL

TRAVERSAYNES, *n.f.pl.* (transverse) flutes; 51:20

TRESBUCHIER, *infin.* of *intr.v.* to fall (over); 11:7: TREBUCHIEZ *past part.pl.*; 43:34

TRESDONT, *adv.* since; 25:66

TRESHASTIS, *a.m.s.* hasty; 58:7: *a.m.pl.*; 91:16

TRESLORS, *adv.* even then, straightway; 61:10

TRESPAS, *n.m.pl.* deaths; 59:35

TRESPASSE, *3rd s.pr.ind.* of *intr.v.* TRESPASSER to die; 49:25

TRESTOURNÉ, *past part.* of *tr.v.* TRESTOURNER to spoil, upset, change; 72:9

TRESTOUT, *adv.* absolutely; 65:8

TREUVE, see TRUIS

TRICHIER, *infin.* of *intr.v.* to cheat; 14:11

TRISTOR, *n.f.s.* grief, affliction; 34:21

TRUIS, *1st s.pr.ind.* of *tr.v.* TROVER to find; 11:19; 77:14: TREUVE *3rd s.pr.ind.*; 65:20

TUIT, *a.m.pl.* all; 48:20; 59:10

UEIL, *n.m.s.* eye; 79:9

UI, see HUI

UMBRE, *n.f.s.* shade, shadow; 77:7

UNG, *a.m.s.* one; 77:1, etc.

USANCE: D'USANCE as a custom; 89:9

USÉ, *past part.* of *tr.v.* USER to wear out; 82:3

VAINT, *3rd s.pr.ind.* of *tr.v.* VAINTRE to vanquish; 16:33

VARIENCE, *n.f.s.* caprice, fickleness; 40:23

VASSELAGE, *n.m.s.* valour, prowess; 59:38

VAURROIE, *3rd s.condit.* of *tr.v.* VALOIR to be worth; 20:45: VAUSIST *3rd s.imperf.subj.*; 45:27

VENDREZ, *2nd pl.fut.* of *intr.v.* VENIR to come; 80:16

VENENEUSE, *a.f.s.* poisonous; 27:1

VENIN, *n.m.s.* poison; 27:10; 54:10

VËOIR, *infin.* of *tr.v.* to see; 10:3; 17:1, etc. (VIR; 53:21): VOYE *1st s.pr.subj.*; 67:17; 68:29; 75:3; 83:13; 96:2: VI *1st s.past def.*; 6:8

VERDOUR, *n.f.s.* verdure; 74:11

VERGUS, *n.m.s.* verjuice (acid liquor from sour grapes, crab-apples, etc.); 56:22

VERMEILLETTE/VERMILLETE, *a.f.s.* red; 37:13; 60:4

VERS, *a.m.pl.* green; 60:6

VESTÉS, *imp. 2nd pl.* of *tr.v.* VESTIR to dress; 50:23: VESTUS *past part.*; 56:15

VI, see VËOIR

VIAIRE, *n.m.s.* face; 15:7; 19:4; 25:33; 26:19

VIC/VIS, *1st s.pr.ind.* of *intr.v.* VIVRE to live; 42:8; 60:39

VIEL, see VUEIL

VIELE, *n.f.s.* hurdy-gurdy; 51:17

VIF/VIFS, *1st s.pr.ind.* of *intr.v.* VIVRE to live; 74:7; 79:4

VIR, see VËOIR

VIS(i)/VIZ, *n.m.s.* face; 2:20; 5:30; 10:11; 16:16; 26:10; 60:3; 84:10: VIS À VIS face to face; 20:14: VIS(ii) *a.m.s.* alive; 10:9

VO, *poss.pron. (2nd pl.)* your; 6:23; 10:11; 24:3, etc.: VOS; 10:7

VOEILLIÉS, see VUEIL

VOIR/VOYRE, *a.* true: À DIRE VOIR to tell the truth; 44:6: AU VOIR PARLER; 1:9: POUR DIRE VOIR; 91:3: VOIR in truth; 41:3; 47:23: VOIRE; 61:3: POUR VOIR; 20:6; 46:9

VOIS, *1st s.pr.ind.* of *intr.v.* ALLER to go; 99:3: VOISE *1st s.pr.subj.*; 63:16: VOISSES *2nd s.pr.subj.*; 35:5: VOIST *3rd s.pr.subj.*; 56:8

VOLAGE, *a.m.s.* flighty; 30:32

VOYE, *n.f.s.* way; 67:6; 68:27; 69:19

VOYRE, see VOIR

VUEIL/VIEL, *1st s.pr.ind.* of *tr.v.* VOLOIR to wish, want; 14:9; 15:16; 47:20, etc.: VEULT *3rd s.pr.ind.*; 87:26: VOEILLIÉS *2nd pl.pr subj.*; 34:11; 38:7: VOULU *1st s.past def.*; 86:38: VOULDROYENT *3rd pl.condit.*; 90:7

VUEILLANCE, *n.f.s.* will, wish; 89:23

VUIDIER, *infin.* of *intr.v.* to leave, empty; 31:13

WACARME, *n.m.s. & int.* war! (Flemish war cry); 34:15; 34:18

YEX, see IEX

YRAIGNE, *n.f.s.* spider; 54:10

YRE, see IRE

YSTROIT, *3rd s.condit.* of *intr.v.* YSSIR to come out; 77:28

YVER, *n.m.s.* Winter; 100:1; 100:9

INDEX OF PROPER NAMES

The number preceding the colon is the item number of the poem; the number following it is the line number.

INDEX OF NAMES

SEMIRAMIS, Semiramis, queen of Assyria, one of the Nine Heroines, 59–23
SOCRATÈS, Socrates, Greek philosopher, 30:24

THESEÜS, Theseus, hero of Greek mythology, 18:1; 29:2; 29:11
THOLOMEÜS, Ptolemy, Egyptian astronomer, 59:7
THOMAS... PIZAIN, Thomas de Pisan, father of Christine de Pisan, 57:14–15
TRISTAIN, Tristan, hero of Celtic and French romance, 28:2

ULIXÈS, Ulysses, Greek hero, 17:2

VALOIS, Bailli de, Eustache Deschamps, 50:18
VENUS, Venus, goddess of love, 17:19
VIRGILLE/VREGILE, Vergil, Latin poet, 36:8; 59:15

YNDES, Les, The Indies, 18:18
YPOCRAS, 'le bon phisicïen'; Hippocrates, Greek doctor, 59:4

ALPHABETICAL INDEX OF
FIRST LINES

The forms of the poems are indicated by the following abbreviations: B (ballade), BD (ballade double), DB (double ballade), CR (chanson royal), R (rondeau), RB (rondeau-ballade), V (virelai). Poems whose first lines are printed in italic type are included among the musical examples.